YOUR NEXT SIX FIGURES

Reveal and Heal Your Way to Receiving and Holding Your Next Six Figure Year, Launch or Month — Without the Sabotage

NATASHA LEIGH BRAY

First published in 2023
by Bray House Publishing

ISBN: 978-1-3999-7547-6

A CIP catalogue record for this book is available
from the British Library.

Illustrations: Property of Natasha Bray Ltd.

To my soulmate, Blake, and my beautiful children, Jenson and Oscar, for showing me over and over again that I do get to have love and success.

CONTENTS

INTRODUCTION

You might have picked up this book because you have been feeling stuck in your business for a while now (even if you have already made six or seven figures), but it's more than just feeling stuck—you have a big desire for more success. You feel in your soul that you are meant for more, and you know deep down you are still playing small, sacrificing or sabotaging yourself.

You are grateful for the success you have already had. But, despite all of the work you've already done, and all of the coaches, courses, and strategies you've invested in, things are just not moving forward the way you expected.

Maybe you are stuck at an income plateau and you just can't seem to earn more than that one certain figure every month. (Yep, been there.)

Maybe you find yourself getting into huge arguments with your partner every time you start seeing more success in your business. (Been there, too!)

Maybe you repeatedly have an empty bank account at the end of every month, despite sometimes earning tens or even hundreds of thousands in monthly revenue. (More common than you think!)

And when you see others skyrocketing their financial success, some who feel like 'newbies' compared to your OG status, it's hard not to compare yourself. That's when the feelings that you really don't want to feel come. The feelings of 'not enoughness'. The feelings of failure. The feelings of unworthiness.

To compensate, you hustle a little (or a lot!) harder. You invest in yet another business or marketing course. And maybe you even question if there is something wrong with you. One thing I can promise is that there isn't anything wrong with you. What you are experiencing is completely normal, and the reason why I can say this so confidently is because every single one of the thousands of female entrepreneurs I have worked with over the years has experienced the same thing, whether they are making hundreds or millions (myself included!).

In your heart and soul, you know there is so much more potential you have left to fulfil—unbelievable success that would make this business journey feel like it is finally giving you the freedom you really came into business for. A part of you knows it is possible to achieve financial freedom and an overflow of abundance, all while doing what you love and changing lives. There *is* a way that you can do all of this while still having plenty of time—time to spend with the ones you love and time to spend all that money you have (deservedly) earned.

But let's be completely honest: there are many emotional and psychological reasons why women sabotage themselves, their businesses, and their potential to receive more wealth and success. Not only that, but there are a whole host of hidden ways these manifest and show up in our lives. And this is where I come in.

I am incredibly passionate about empowering women to achieve unbelievable levels of wealth and success, for themselves and their families. I truly believe that anything and everything is possible for those who decide to go all in on changing their lives.

All of this begins with the elusive six-figure success that has (rightly or wrongly) become a popular marker of you 'making it' in the entrepreneurial space. Whether your next milestone for your business is a six-figure year, launch or month, this book will show you a different way to get there, with a lot more ease and a lot less sabotage than the way you are currently doing things. It will be your guide on how to navigate every new level you reach, and it is something you can come back to time and time again…

Because I have a secret to share with you:

No financial milestone will ever be enough if you don't feel 'enough'. You will hit those milestones you dreamed of and feel empty inside, if you haven't built a life you love too. It's not just about hustling every hour of your day, making the money, and spending it all on bills, coaches, or the next shiny object; it's about keeping more of the money you make, too. It's about rewriting the financial and emotional legacies of the women who came before us. It's about building true success and wealth for our future, and for the next generations. It's about making an overflow of money, while having deeply connected relationships and living a life you love. Because there is absolutely zero point in having all that money if you have no time to spend it and nobody to spend it with! It's about making those six-figure leaps on repeat, without the fear that everything else will collapse around you. It's about turning that money into a life that is rich in all of the ways.

Your financial evolution and your emotional evolution go hand in hand. They are divinely intertwined. They are also (surprisingly) deeply linked to your spiritual evolution, as you will see as you make your way through this book.

The women who have unlocked emotional, financial, and spiritual freedom are not just rich; they are revolutionary.

If you are catching yourself nodding along with everything you are reading, thinking, 'Yes, Natasha!' then you are in the right place. This book will totally change your life. All the books, courses, coaches, and strategies you have already invested in have contributed to your journey and brought you to where you are right now (even if that journey didn't look exactly how you hoped it would). One of the most important initial steps in this next step in your journey is to acknowledge and show gratitude for that, rather than beating yourself up for 'not making the most of previous investments' or 'not making the right investments'. Because the truth is, there is no such thing as mistakes; only lessons. I believe this so deeply that I make a point of wiring it into my clients' minds so they believe it, too. Some of my greatest successes have come from my greatest 'mistakes'. They have come from when I've decided to look at the lessons and the blessings behind them instead of making them mean something about me. Were they ever truly mistakes if they have led to such valuable insights and positives? It is all a matter of perspective.

Why Your Next Six Figures Hasn't Happened Yet

The real reason you are feeling stuck and haven't quite unlocked that next six figures (yet!) is you've spent a lot of time, money, and energy looking outside of yourself for success, instead of looking at where it really comes from—and that's inside! You have been led to believe that the answer to unlocking your next six figures is found in an external source. Yet, whilst practical strategy is absolutely a critical piece of the overall 'success' puzzle, I've discovered that it isn't actually the most important one. If it were, we would all be celebrating our six-figure years/months/days constantly like it was a piece of cake, right?

The truth is, you don't have a strategy problem—you have a sabotage problem. The real answers lie inside you; hiding beneath something I call your Success Saboteur Archetypes (commonly shortened to in this book and my work as Success Saboteurs). There are five universal Success Saboteur Archetypes that come up to 'protect' (i.e. prevent) you from making those big scary financial leaps, even though you want to make them so much.

After you have read this book and unveiled your own hidden wounds and Success Saboteurs (with my guidance), you will have experienced profound shifts that will allow you to stop the sabotage—stop playing small—and finally be that woman who gets to unlock her next six figures with so much more ease.

And although this book is about unlocking your next six figures, the work that you will do here does not *just* influence your relationship with money; it influences every single relationship in your life. Why? Because once you heal what is really at the root of your Success Saboteurs, you are transformed and opened up to receiving on every level—not just the financial level. You become the woman who is able to have it all; the next six-figure milestone, the loving partnership, the dream home, the two-point-four children—whatever 'having it all' means to you (and there's no right or wrong answer here as everyone is so different). Most importantly, you become the woman who can hold it all too.

By the end of this book, if you do the powerful, healing work, you will see changes in every area of your life. It's very normal for you to come into my world and quantum leap your income to the best revenue months you've ever had. It's normal to find yourself selling every day (with so much more ease), feeling closer to your partner than you ever have (or attracting one!), feeling a confidence and inner peace you've never felt before, and magnetising more clients than ever—and all whilst looking in the mirror and truly, deeply loving the woman you see there.

I know you have been raised to work hard and achieve your way to wealth and success. This hustling, hard work and sacrifice may have gotten you some success, but it won't get you to your next six figures. Or if it does, this success won't be sustainable, and you'll experience a big crash afterwards.

I know; I've been there. I've lived it and I have learned the hard way.

The most important lesson I have learned is that you don't just achieve your next six figures, you receive it. And after that, you need to be able to hold it. A combination of both receiving and achieving leads to that next six-figure leap you have on your vision board. Then, having the confidence and resilience to hold it, no matter what life or business throws your way, is essential to consistent financial success and growth (without the sabotage). You need to become the woman who is able to receive and hold her next six figures. Otherwise, it will come flying in and then go flying straight back out again, and you'll find yourself right back at square one.

Why This Book?

Sadly, statistics show the majority of women-led businesses (88%) make less than six figures in revenue, and less than 2% of women-led businesses reach the seven-figure mark (with men being five times more likely to achieve this).[1] And this gender gap increases significantly when we bring ethnicity into the equation too.

Well, not in my world. I want to change that—for me and for you. I refuse to be another statistic. You get to change that, too, and it all begins with the belief that it is possible for you.

As much as everyone tries to be modest and 'spiritual' and to say it's 'not about the money', I want to tell you: it absolutely is about the money! And there's no shame in admitting that. In fact, the more you say you don't want money, the more you subconsciously push it away.

It has to be about the money, because without the money, you can't continue making the world-changing impact you are here to make. Without the money, you may end up having to go back to a job you hate and give up on your soul purpose entirely—and I don't know about you, but I am totally unemployable now, so that's just not an option!

Most of all, without the money, you can't contribute to your family's income or education costs for your children, treat yourself and your loved ones to holidays and experiences, buy your dream home or pay off your mortgage early, retire your partner, donate to charitable causes close to your heart or [insert thing you wish you could pay for here], can you?

So, *yes*—the money *is* important. (It feels good to acknowledge it, right?) The money is your reward for your service and the impact you are making. But, more importantly, it's about time the world had more rich women in it. More women with more money is a powerful legacy to leave

---

[1]Alison Rose Review:
https://assets.publishing.service.gov.uk/media/5c8147e2e5274a2a595bb24a/RoseReview_Digital_FINAL.PDF

the next generations with. More rich women means a richer world, in so many ways. More rich women means a world where there is greater safety and security available to more women and children.

A six-figure yearly revenue can be lifechanging for a woman. Six figures in profit? Even better. Six-figure launches and six-figure months? What a reward for your impact! Every woman deserves to find her seven-figure body of work (the one that will not only make millions, but also impact millions!).

You only have to Google 'making six figures' for hundreds of books to appear, but this book—the one you're reading right now—takes a wildly different approach to six-figure success.

Why Me?

If you are new to my world: I'm Natasha Leigh Bray, a Success Mastery Coach, Healer, Business Mentor & Teacher to high achievers, healers and leaders who have a deep desire to change their world and the world. Yes, I am one of that 2% who has reached seven figure years in my business. Yes, I am an abuse and domestic violence survivor. And yes, I was diagnosed with attention deficit hyperactivity disorder (ADHD) aged thirty-five. I am a Gemini and 4/1 Manifesting Generator, for those of you interested in astrology and human design. I am an introverted, 'average' smalltown girl who somehow managed to evolve into a global leader impacting women across seventy countries worldwide, with a gift of changing lives in as little as one healing session. I am a wisdom seeker, a psychic, a spiritual teacher, a mother, a partner, a daughter and an eternal learner changing the world in my own unique way. But I do not define myself by any of those things.

Who I really am, is just Natasha—a woman who wakes up every day with a deep desire to leave the world better than when I entered it.

This book is a huge part of making that happen. I have kept this body of work to my small corner of the Internet for three and a half years. It's time for it to reach and transform more women just like you.

I'm not just a coach who has learned about this transformation; I have lived it. Since being a fresh-faced, super-introverted seventeen-year-old in 2004, I have committed myself to a world class, lifelong education and career dedicated to transforming lives and helping others, underpinned by evidence-based psychology and real-world experience. You won't find what you read here in any other book. This knowledge comes from my extensive professional knowledge and background, combined with my lived wisdom of overcoming my own Success Saboteur Archetypes and from the front row tickets I have had to all of the subconscious secrets in the minds and hearts of the incredible women entrepreneurs in my world.

My work is based on research by women, about women, for women, and it has been written by a woman. This book won't be like any business book you've ever read—and it goes deep. It's going to take you to places you probably haven't been to before. You will experience lightbulb moment after lightbulb moment, and finally, so much of who you are and why you are holding yourself back will finally make sense.

Whenever I have reached a new level in my business, I have worked on my Success Saboteurs so I can ensure that I can receive and hold my next six figures whilst holding love and life and mothering two young children.

Between 2020 and 2023, over seven thousand five hundred women were impacted by my free online Success Saboteur Archetypes Assessment, and thousands more have been impacted by my live experiences and courses.

This work truly comes from my heart and soul, as well as my professional experience and brilliant mind.

Before we dive in, I want to tell you briefly about my background, just in case you are thinking I had a special head start that would make it natural for me to effortlessly uplevel my life and my business.

I had a childhood of chronic abuse, bullying, and poverty. I lived in one of the roughest council estates[2] in my hometown: Bridgend, South Wales, in the United Kingdom. I always felt like I didn't belong. I never felt safe, and the love and financial security I wanted was not available to me. I spent many years 'hidden homeless', meaning I had no secure or stable home and sofa surfed with family or friends when I wasn't in temporary university accommodation.

No childhood (and no parent) is perfect and I have found peace with my past, but it's safe to say I never felt loved, safe or wanted, and felt completely alone in the world. For a long time, I had zero self-worth or confidence and I was desperate to find love.

It's no surprise, then, that I ended up in a string of abusive relationships—ones that were coercively controlling; ones where I was cheated on and one where I was almost killed. One Christmas, in my early twenties, my ex-partner's best friend walked in on a life-threatening situation and saved me.

---

[2]A council estate is government housing in the UK, the equivalent of 'the projects' in the US or 'social housing' in Australia.

As traumatic as it was, this was one of thoşe pivotal 'wakeup call' moments where I knew my life had to change. I knuckled down hard on changing others' lives—and it changed mine.

Whilst I certainly partied and studied hard at university, I also spent my spare time doing breakfast runs for the homeless rough sleepers in my hometown and being a support worker for Victim Support, a charity that helps people who have been impacted by crime. I became a double-award-winning psychology, criminology, and social work graduate and a published researcher by the age of twenty-four. I was developing and leading lifesaving, transformational initiatives in homelessness services at the tender age of twenty-five, and I have been awarded a fellowship for my contribution to the healing industry.

I have become a pioneer in every career path I have ever entered (including in my businesses). As a multi-award-winning coach and healer recognised as one of the top thirty-five leaders in Great Britain, I now work globally with thousands of women per year to reveal and heal the Success Saboteurs that have been limiting their financial, emotional, and spiritual success. My approach is 'the perfect blend of the science and the woo', as my clients say.

I also train other therapists, psychologists, healers and even doctors in my innovative methods, and they comment on how my methods generate the most transformational and rapid results they have ever seen in their own clients (despite some having decades' worth of certifications and experience in other world-renowned therapies!).

My Six-Figure Journey

I started my first business in 2014. By August of 2017, I'd left my social work career to go all in on my business after having my first child. There is nothing like seeing the world through a mother's eyes to make you look at all of the wounds you've been trying to bury and finally work on them so you can be the best mother you can be.

At the time, my business was turning over a few thousand pounds a month, and I thought to myself, 'If I can just make this into a six-figure business, that will be enough.' Well, the Universe had other ideas! I didn't just make it to a six-figure business. My first six-figure year happened in 2018. By 2020, I had a seven-figure business and by 2021, I had a multi-seven-figure business. I couldn't believe it. At the time of writing, I have consecutively received six or multi six figures each month for over three years now.

Back in 2017, when I left my social work career, I was trying desperately to reach that six-figure year. A six-figure year is a key milestone for many different people, especially in the coaching and entrepreneurial spaces. Some people put that goal on a pedestal. After all, a six-figure business gives you enough profit to live a comfortable life, and that was all I ever really wanted. As a social worker, I'd only ever earned £33,000 a year, so six figures in one year felt like a lot of money.

Not only have I made six figures in a month, but I have also made six figures in a day!

Honestly, that kind of money is crazy to me, and it took ages for it to truly sink in and for me to see that it was real.

My six-figure journey took me from quitting my social work job as a single mum on minimum wage and tax credits, to becoming an unexpected cash millionaire in a matter of just a few years. Every time I hit a new milestone, I felt like I was doing it for women everywhere, not just for me.

My biggest achievement though is buying my beautiful forever home for me and my family. It's our little haven, on three acres of land and surrounded by fields as far as the eye can see. We have a huge vegetable patch and a bounty of homegrown food and wild berries every year. I see the sunrise in my back garden every morning, squirrels and rabbits running around. Our resident woodpecker pops by most days too. It really is magical. My children love it. I love it. It means so much to my inner child that we finally have a safe, secure home and it is better than I could have ever dreamed of.

I share this because I want you to know that whatever you have been through, wherever you have come from and wherever you may be right now, you can overcome it, and you can have unbelievable success in your business and life. Where you came from doesn't have to determine where you go.

I'll be sharing my story of my own wounding and Success Saboteur Archetypes along the way, but please don't see me as a victim. I have chosen to use my story and my past for good; to turn the proverbial shit into gold; to shine a light on the shadows that are keeping you stuck in your business and life. Too many women spend their whole lives believing their self-sabotage is normal; that they have no wounds impacting them. Consequently, they settle for less than they truly deserve. I don't want that to be you. If you want a different result, you've got to take a different approach.

There have been a lot of six-figure leaps I have made along my journey, and I am looking forward to sharing with you how you can make your next six-figures too. I will take you to your first six-figure year, to your first six-figure launch, to your first six-figure month, and maybe even to your first six-figure day—no matter where you are in your journey. My clients have repeatedly unlocked six-figure years, six-figure launches, six-figure months and even six-figure clients without necessarily learning more strategy. In fact, they often have to 'unlearn' a lot of the strict strategy rules that were keeping them stuck in 'hustle, struggle, and sacrifice' mode.

My Promise to You

When you finish this book and all of the healing gold inside, you will not be the same woman you were when you started it—in the best possible way. These pages combine both the practical and the magical for an unforgettable life- and business-changing experience that will make your next six figures a lot more possible. It really is like getting a degree in you.

Across the chapters in this book, I will take you deeper into the Success Saboteur Archetypes than I have ever done before outside of my paid courses.

- You will experience deep healing around the Success Saboteurs that will leave you with a new sense of inner and outer freedom.
- You will create your action plan for how you are going to receive, achieve and hold your next six figures, without your life or

business crashing down around you.

- You will take action along the way that will create immediate results in your external world.

This isn't to say that everything you want in life will just suddenly land in your lap (you still need to do the work!), but you will start to recognise the fact that you are currently making things much more difficult than they need to be, and you will discover how to make these things much easier to navigate.

Awareness is the first stage of change. Get ready for so many breakthroughs as you come to understand why you are sabotaging yourself and what you can do to change that (so you can receive with a lot more ease).

The shifts you will experience will be visible – not just in your business, but in every relationship in your life (especially your relationship with money).

How does that sound?

Are you ready to unlock what it really takes to have six-figure leaps on repeat, without sabotage, hustle, and sacrifice? If so, get cosy, grab a pen and a journal, and let's begin what is likely to be the biggest transformational journey of your life to date. Turning this page to the next chapter of this book is synonymous with you turning the corner in your business that you've been subconsciously too scared to go around.

This work can bring up some strong emotions. Specifically, it will bring up all those things you have buried that your next six figures are currently hiding behind. To support you with feeling safe as you dig deep into this work, you can download my Safe Success Imprint Audio at www.natashabray.com/book-resources, which you can listen to daily to soothe your subconscious and soul as we embark on this journey together.

There are also some important links to resources and charities at the back of the book that may help you if you have been affected by any of the topics mentioned in this book.

You are going to have so many revelations about why you've been holding yourself back, and the only possible outcome from these revelations will be you taking action in a whole new way. The work that you do here will be key to unlocking your next six figures and unveiling the Revolutionary Woman you already are beneath your Success Saboteurs.

You were born ready. Let's do this!

Love Natasha x

P.S. Keep in touch while you are reading this book; I am here for you and cannot wait to hear all about your 'aha' moments and successes.

Instagram: @natashaleighbray

Facebook: @natashabraycoach

LinkedIn: natashaleighbray

YouTube: @natashaleighbray

Download your book bonuses here:

www.natashabray.com/book-resources

1

THE SUCCESS SABOTEUR ARCHETYPES

In the coming chapters, you will learn about the specific Success Saboteur Archetypes (and what to do about them) in great detail, but first I want to give you an overview of what they are and how they are collectively blocking your next six figures.

There are two key parts of your mind: the conscious and the subconscious. The conscious mind is the rational and logical part of our brain behind how we operate our everyday activities. It contains the thoughts, feelings and memories we are aware of at any given moment. Then there's your subconscious mind: the thoughts, feelings, fears, beliefs and memories outside of our conscious awareness.

Your Success Saboteurs are psychological constructs or 'archetypes' that live in your subconscious mind and influence your patterns of thoughts, your feelings and behaviours in every relationship in your life, including your relationship with yourself, others and money. They influence your energy, and your energy influences your business. They are the reason you sabotage yourself with receiving and holding more of the things you consciously want. Their number one job is to keep you safe from anything you (rightly or wrongly) believe is going to hurt you or potentially cause you pain.

And, unfortunately, the subconscious mind is more powerful than the conscious and always wins—no matter what you consciously want! This then impacts *if* or *how* you take action on a strategy and ultimately how successful that strategy will be for you.

So, you want the next six figures, more success, more sales, more clients… I hear you. That's what your conscious mind wants. You know what you need to do. But you are not doing it or are not getting the success with the ease and speed you expected because your subconscious Success Saboteurs are in conflict with your conscious mind. This cognitive dissonance can leave you feeling confused, beating yourself up, and a deep sense of shame over why you know the strategy but you just cannot seem to take the action you need to take to reach your goals.

Let me give you another example:

You really need to bring more income in to cover the bills this month. Like, *really*. You put a plan together for how to make it happen. You sit down to start implementing the plan and faff about scrolling through social media, fiddling with your website or Canva images and, before you know it, the day is over, you are picking the kids up from school, and you have got literally *nothing* done off your To Do list. You put the children to bed, beat yourself up and pour yourself a glass of wine while you Netflix-binge the evening away to make you 'feel' better—and take zero action in your business. (Yep, I've been there too!)

Your conscious mind is saying, 'I need to make money!' but one of the Success Saboteur Archetypes in your subconscious is saying, 'You're not worthy of that money!' or 'It's not safe to receive that money!'

The result? You could win a Guinness World Record for procrastination. You stay stuck.

When my clients come to me, we find that their big goals and dreams (conscious mindset) are often in a battle with their Success Saboteurs (subconscious mindset)—and it is *this* conflict caused by the two parts of our mindset that stops us achieving the success we want. We *want* success, but deep down, on the subconscious level, we don't believe or feel we are safe to receive it, that we deserve it, or that it is even possible for us. You must address both your conscious and subconscious mind if you want to unlock your next six figures without the sabotage. Because your subconscious holds the hidden insights into what is really holding you back and leads to the most powerful change. If there's one thing I've learned, it is never what you think it is consciously, and this can only be accessed with therapeutic tools that access the subconscious state (you will be directed to my powerful subconscious work later in the book after we work through the conscious layers first).

It goes a lot deeper than just conscious and subconscious mindset, though, because both layers of beliefs are just symptoms of a deeper root cause.

Where Do Your Success Saboteurs Actually Come From?

Your Success Saboteur Archetypes are actually 'protectors' that develop in response to wounds of your heart that are caused by experiences of trauma in childhood.

When you hear the word 'trauma', your mind might immediately go to *Big T* trauma, such as abuse, death or loss of a parent, or a serious accident. But most traumas that contribute to our Success Saboteur Archetypes developing are actually something we call *Little t* traumas; these are universal, meaning everyone is likely to have experienced them in one way or another. *Little t* traumas can be anything that made us feel rejected or betrayed, judged, unsafe, not accepted, abandoned, not worthy, not loved or not enough in some way.

Everyone has felt one of these feelings at some point in their lives—though we minimise or deny or forget what we've experienced as we grow older. However, although we might deny or forget, the trauma imprint remains there, affecting us, closing off our hearts, causing us to sabotage ourselves and affecting our ability to receive and hold our next six figures. As world-renowned trauma expert Gabor Maté so aptly says, 'Trauma is not what happens to you, it is what happens inside you as a result of what happened to you.' I actually prefer to use the term 'wounds'.

For example, maybe you were laughed at when you read something wrong in front of your class at school. Perhaps you were wrongly accused and shamed for cheating in an exam or lying to a parent. Maybe you were always compared to an older sibling and never felt good enough. Maybe you had to move schools a lot and lost all your friends in the process.

What's really interesting is that, according to epigenetics (the study of how your behaviours and environment can impact gene expression), we don't just carry our own trauma imprints: we may also be genetically and energetically carrying the wounding of up to seven generations before us!

These can be carried with us, and passed down from generation to generation.

This cycle continues until a cycle breaker is born; someone who steps up to break the cycle and change the legacy forever—for themselves and for their future generations—replacing those trauma imprints with something I call Success Imprints!

If you picked up this book, *that's you*! *You* are the Legacy Maker. That's why you are drawn to my work. That's why you're reading these words.

These trauma imprints are at the root of our Success Saboteurs. They are the reason our Success Saboteurs exist. Through my work, I have found that these trauma imprints are not just stored in our minds, they are also stored in our hearts and cause us to put energetic walls up to protect our hearts from having the pain of that wound or trauma triggered again. These energetic walls don't only block the pain, however; they block the good, too. A wall is a wall, after all: it blocks *everything* coming in (even the good).

Those walls? They also stop things getting out, namely your heart energy, which has a magnetic energetic frequency thousands of times stronger than your mind[3]. That incredible heart energy is the number one thing that makes you magnetic to receiving more love, success and abundance. The more your heart is healed, the more you expand your capacity to receive and hold more, and the more magnetic you become.

The heart has long been recognised as important in ancient wisdom and eastern culture, yet, somewhere along the way, the brain and mindset became more important in modern research and western approaches to

---

[3] Science of the Heart: Exploring the Role of the Heart in Human Performance, Volume 2, by Rollin McCraty, Ph.D. Director of Research, HeartMath Research Center, p. 36. Published by HeartMath Institute, 2015, ISBN 9781513606361.

transformation.

In the womb, your heart develops before your brain. And there is incredible research to support that your heart actually communicates with your mind (not the other way around)[4]. So, it then makes complete sense that I have seen huge and rapid shifts in my own and clients' successes when also healing on the heart level.

I like to think of the Success Saboteurs as guardians of your heart, and their number one job is to keep your heart safe from feeling the pain of those past wounds. Ironically, they think they are helping you as they did many times throughout your childhood, but they are actually limiting you now because you don't need them in the same way anymore.

When we heal the heart, we impact everything—we change the signals being sent to the Success Saboteurs and break down the energetic walls your heart has created for protection that were also blocking you from receiving. So, you feel safer and freer internally to take fast action and implement the strategies that will bring more success—and your heart is more open to receiving that success.

So, as you can now see, it is so important to move beyond strategy *and* mindset when it comes to receiving and holding your next six figures. We especially need to consider the most powerful influence on it all—the heart.

---

[4] This finding came from the same paper by Rollin McCraty referenced previously.

Meet Your Success Saboteur Archetypes

I discovered that there are five universal Success Saboteur Archetypes guarding the hearts of female entrepreneurs and holding them back from their full potential. We all have all five Success Saboteurs; however, each of us will have a primary one—one that is our key Success Saboteur; one that is always our biggest protector when we feel unsafe or face stress, challenges, and hurdles—in life and business. Every new level I grow to in my own business journey, I uncover new insights on how they show up, and so my unique body of work around this is continuously evolving as I evolve.

Allow me to briefly introduce you to them and how they are each impacting you receiving and holding your next six figures.

The Overprotector Success Saboteur

The Overprotector is keeping you stuck, going round in circles and only ever earning 'safe money' or achieving 'safe success' in your business. Your next six-figure leap is currently hiding behind your comfort zone thanks to this Success Saboteur. Receiving and holding extraordinary levels of money and success does not come from playing in your comfort zone. When you heal this, you are able to feel safe to receive and hold more success than others around you.

The Overgiver Success Saboteur

The Overgiver is keeping you stuck in cycles of undercharging, overgiving, putting everyone else before yourself and struggling to implement the boundaries you need to receive and hold more clients, more income and more success. Your next six-figure leap is hiding behind people pleasing thanks to this Success Saboteur. You will struggle to charge enough, have enough or feel enough until you heal it.

The Imposter Success Saboteur

The Imposter keeps you stuck by killing your creativity and your ability to take the most successful money generating actions in your business. Your million-dollar business idea is often *hiding* behind the Imposter Success Saboteur; you just haven't trusted it enough to take action on it! When you heal this, you stop giving your power away to others and do business your way (which is the most successful way, by the way!).

The Outcast Success Saboteur

The Outcast is blocking your ability to be seen more, sell more and scale more. It's so much more than visibility issues. It blocks your money, sales and marketing and keeps any group experiences you launch plateaued in terms of your income and how many clients you can hold at any one time.

The Hustler Success Saboteur

The Hustler is the main reason why it may seem like you cannot receive success in your business or bank account without sabotaging yourself, your health or your relationships. Healing this will allow you to let go of hard work and struggle and receive and keep more money than you ever thought possible, working less and having more time for love, health and fun (yes, you do get to have it all!).

Although we each have a Primary Success Saboteur (you can do my quick online assessment to discover yours at www.natashabray.com/success-saboteur-archetype), you may notice that a different one may also be stronger at different times in your life based on the 'thing' you subconsciously feel you need protection from.

As examples, you might be offered a huge opportunity to speak on a stage, but your Outcast might come to the surface. A friend might display jealousy around your business, which triggers your Overprotector into action. Or you might have a bad experience with a wrong-fit client or team member and your Overprotector comes up to protect you from it ever happening again.

Revealing and healing just one of your Success Saboteurs can have a profound impact on you, your relationships, and your business, but healing all five is the secret sauce to becoming the Revolutionary Woman who can receive and hold her next six figures without the sabotage—the woman who can truly receive and hold it all.

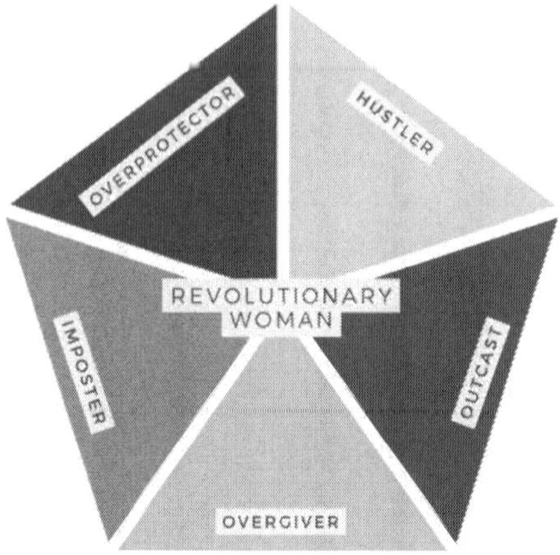

Figure 1: The Success Saboteurs Archetypes

Your Success Saboteurs Impact If and How You Take Action

The deep beliefs and feelings behind our Success Saboteurs—specifically around not being safe, enough, capable, worthy or deserving—can become a self-fulfilling prophecy. You must believe and feel on a deep level that you can be, do, and have the things you want and that it is safe for you to have them. If you don't, you won't take action—or you'll sabotage yourself and take action that's not aligned or has no power behind it and, unsurprisingly, does not get results.

Let me give you an example. Someone enquires about working with you. They send you a message asking about your services. You do one of the following:

1. Don't respond, because you've already *made enough money this month* and you feel guilty or bad for making more than other

people you know (the Overprotector);

2. Procrastinate over replying and go into spirals of self-doubt (because part of your mind is asking, 'Why would they even want to work with me? I am not going to be able to help them') (the Imposter);
3. Get on a long sales call where you end up coaching them for free and then offering a reduced rate, and then they don't sign up with you anyway, leaving you feeling resentful and frustrated (the Overgiver);
4. Avoid them entirely and refuse to get on a call because you *cannot bear to sell* to them and worry the call may lead to a 'no' anyway (the Outcast);
5. Respond right away and fit them into your family or personal time (again), because you are already overbooked and spend the money straight back out again (the Hustler); or
6. Confidently tell them how you can help them, give them your full rate, follow up until you secure the sale, and book them into your next available time slot during dedicated working hours.

Honestly, now, which one are you?

Whatever category you fall into, your Success Saboteur Archetypes have impacted how and if you take action and have directly impacted the amount of success you have been able to receive and hold as a result.

With these five Success Saboteurs showing up and sabotaging the huge goals so many women entrepreneurs have, this book has been written not *just* on making your next six figures… This book is about far more than that.

It's About the Legacy You Live and Leave

The Revolutionary Woman doesn't just make money. She builds wealth. She is a Legacy Maker. She rewrites the negative legacies of those who came before her and lives and leaves a new legacy for herself and the future generations. She changes her world and *the* world from having the courage and the bravery to try something new and different.

Honestly, it breaks my heart that there are so many six-, multi-six- and even seven-figure businesswomen out there working so hard to provide for their families, yet they get to the end of the month with little or nothing left in their bank accounts. Why? Because they sabotage their wealth. There is no point in making your next six figures if you can't hold onto it because you sabotage yourself. I want to teach you how to make six figures, and another six figures, and another six figures after that! I want you to be able to hold it, too.

As we dive deep into each of the five Success Saboteurs from Chapter 3, you will see that each has distinctly different blocks with distinctly different wounding experiences at the root of them, and that each of them shows up in different ways. However, there are some overlaps between them, too. Sometimes healing one can influence healing in the others.

The Success Saboteur Archetypes are intricate and complex in the ways they manifest, but with a brief understanding as to their foundations, we can now move on and explore how we heal them through my five-level healing approach, Success Imprinting. In the next chapter, we will take a look at the five crucial levels of healing of our Success Saboteurs that we need to incorporate to receive and hold more without the sabotage: mind, heart, soul, energy, and action.

2

SUCCESS IMPRINTING: THE FIVE LEVELS OF HEALING

Success Imprinting, my unique model of transformation for revealing and healing the Success Saboteur Archetypes, is the method that underpins all of my work and how my clients and I get such rapid and revolutionary financial results (as well as emotional and spiritual ones). I have identified five levels of healing, all of which beautifully work together to heal your Success Saboteur Archetypes and unlock the Revolutionary Woman within who can receive and hold more success. You can see from the diagram that each of the five levels has multiple elements within it too. It is important to work on all five levels, not only the conscious mindset level that comes with most mindset work, or solely the practical level that is found in the usual 'business course' approaches.

You may have worked in one area, but not really seen a benefit. Or maybe you have done lots of healing before, but still not seen any tangible results in your business.

It's important to understand that each of the different levels compound each other to become something far stronger than anything in isolation.

The idea of Success Imprinting is that we reveal, heal, and replace the trauma imprints that are at the root of the five Success Saboteurs with Success Imprints. This holistic approach sets you free to receive and hold all the success and wealth that you are destined for, and it allows you to unlock your next six figures without sabotage, sacrifice or hustle.

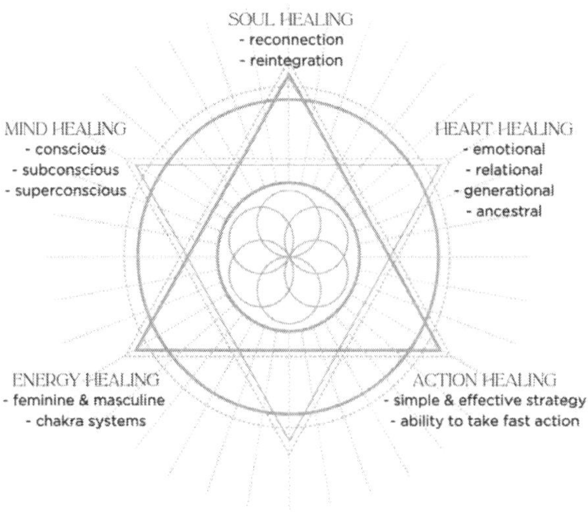

Figure 2: Success Imprinting

Unlocking your next six figures in a sustainable way involves healing your Success Saboteurs on all five of the levels. That deeper mind, heart, soul, energy, and action approach to transformation is unique to my work, and is where I come in. It is my secret sauce for clients who are saying they've had more transformation in one workshop with me than in a lifetime of therapy. I truly believe that healing your Success Saboteur Archetypes is what will really make any strategy work for you, because afterwards, you take action in a completely different way and are open to receiving the results of that action.

The content of this book naturally incorporates all of these levels of healing from a powerful conscious perspective to start to create big shifts for you—bringing the hidden to light. Later in the book, you'll receive a link to a subconscious Success Imprinting session from me—but you'll need to consciously understand and unveil all of the Success Saboteur Archetypes first.

Let me explain the five levels to you in more detail, so you can understand further why strategy may not have been enough and why healing on all levels is so important to your next six figures.

Level 1: Mind Healing

Mind healing involves transforming your beliefs on both a conscious and subconscious level, and opening up access to the superconscious.

You need to see the exact thoughts and feelings and experiences that cause the Success Saboteurs to exist within you, and how they show up in your life right now. How do they show up in your relationships with your parents, partners or children? How do they show up in your business with money, clients and even with your team? How are they showing up with your health and wellbeing? Not forgetting the hidden subconscious ones that can only be accessed with subconscious work! When you do this, you are able to rewire and align both your conscious and subconscious beliefs to support the strategies you are trying to implement, instead of sabotaging them. This is important, because if you don't work on both, you will only have short-term shifts, and you will slip back into old patterns of behaviour. We also tap into the superconscious—a form of higher unconsciousness where all original ideas and innovations that change the world come from (great for accessing your million-dollar business idea!).

Level 2: Heart Healing

Heart healing involves healing the emotional wounds and key life relationships that are at the root of your Success Saboteur Archetypes.

This allows you to feel safe to let down those heart walls and dramatically expand your energetic capacity to receive and hold higher levels of money, success, impact and love. Most people think they have money blocks when in fact they have something I call Receiving Wounds of the heart blocking them from receiving anything—including money. Once these are healed, you take action and use strategies in a more powerful way and can actually receive the money and success that comes from the action, instead of sabotaging it. Only then will you truly be able to open your heart to receiving and holding your next six figures without the sabotage.

The relational and generational aspects of this layer of healing are incredibly important because every relationship that formed a part of our identity can keep triggering us and our Success Saboteur Archetypes to come up to protect us. Even if that person is no longer in your life, every time someone displays similar behaviour, it will activate your Success Saboteur Archetype to protect you until the Root Wounding relationship is healed and the emotion released and neutralised. We can experience heart healing on a conscious level (I will share some tasks with you throughout to help with this), but I have also developed a very powerful subconscious method, very creatively called HeartHealing, that works with the mind-heart connection and rapidly heals the hidden heart wounds in as little as one hour. This is one of the biggest needle movers for my clients, and you will get access to a powerful taster session of this subconscious work later in the book.

Level 3: Soul Healing

I believe parts of our soul break off when we experience a trauma or wound—to protect us from the pain that part of us felt. The soul journey is bringing all of these parts home to ourselves again.

Soul healing is about integrating parts of your soul so you feel whole again, and reconnecting to your higher self and soul purpose. I do this using spiritual techniques to integrate parts of your soul that disconnected at the time the wound was created, and by bringing in your higher self, so you can remember and reintegrate who you really were from birth. We also access soul-led strategy for a divinely guided business and magical growth that defies logic. This is important because we cannot be our whole selves if we are denying our spiritual selves. No amount of money or success will ever be enough if your soul isn't satisfied. Connecting to and integrating our spiritual selves gives us a powerful advantage in business that many are not accessing.

Level 4: Energy Healing

Energy healing is about balancing and unblocking your energy (especially your feminine and masculine energies) for continued receiving and holding of more success.

Energy is everything; it affects how magnetic we are to the things we desire; it affects how people respond to us. When your energy is blocked, things that used to work just don't seem to work anymore. You may even start to see a decline in your income; repelling money rather than making it. Many of the gifts behind the Success Saboteur Archetypes I will introduce you to later are unlocked from within the chakra energy system.

We all have masculine ('doing') energy and feminine ('being') energy regardless of our gender, and the balance of the healed masculine and feminine energies is where people experience the most success and flow, and the least sabotage.

This is important because most people are operating from a wounded feminine or wounded masculine energy that keeps them stuck in their sabotaging patterns. Being too far in your wounded feminine energy means you can become passive, too laid back, and expect success to just 'manifest' or come to you without taking enough action. If you are too far in your wounded masculine energy, you can become too obsessive, hustling, needy, and controlling, and you may be taking lots of action but not the results you expected due to the energy behind it.

Feminine and masculine energies are positively impacted when we heal the relational wounds of the heart impacting them – the relationships with both masculine and feminine that have shaped your identity.

Level 5: Action Healing

Action healing happens when we take aligned action using super-simple soul-led strategies that bring your version of success into reality.

At this level, it's all about unlocking the ability to take fast action on simple strategies and be fearless in trying and learning as you go (trial and error), with the healing allowing you to do business your way; to be creative and innovative with strategies that feel good to you. Following someone else's strategy will never work entirely the same way for you. This is so important because using other people's strategies can leave you feeling burned out and unfulfilled in your business, and will not necessarily be sustainable long-term. But combined with all of the other levels of healing, we are able to get out of our own ways and take action on soul-led strategies that bring huge success that goes beyond any logical, 'normal' business growth.

When all five of these levels are healed and the results begin to compound, this is where the true essence of my work can be seen – what I embody and help other women embody, too – and that is the unlocking of what I call the Revolutionary Woman within. Healing the wounds and unlocking the hidden gifts behind all five Success Saboteur Archetypes makes way for the Revolutionary Woman, who is able to receive, achieve and hold her next six figures (and beyond)—without the sabotage.

When the Revolutionary Woman rises, she is able to easily receive and hold higher levels of success, money, love and happiness, because she has healed the Success Saboteurs and the wounds at the root of them that kept her playing small and safe.

Multidimensional Results

Here is the other bit of juicy info you need to know…

One of my biggest strengths is how highly results focused I am. I have a talent for turning inner healing into phenomenal external tangible results.

Healing your Success Saboteur Archetypes and the heart wounds beneath them using my specific five-level Success Imprinting process won't just make you your next six figures in your business with a lot more ease (although that's a pretty epic outcome in itself!); it transforms *everything* in your life!

Here are all the different areas of your life you can expect to see results in that my clients and I have had results in after doing this work:

Money and Success

You will be able to receive more, make more, and hold more of the money you make—and actually *build wealth* (hello, overflow in your bank accounts every month!). You'll be able to receive and hold higher levels of success in all areas—not just in your business. My client, single mother Olivia, went from $60,000 years and being full of overwhelm and self-doubt to $60,000 *months,* achieving consistent increases in revenue month after month. And the best part is that she now feels *worthy* and is able to spend time with her young son. Having been a single mum myself, I know how truly meaningful that is for them both.

Marketing and Sales

You become a magnetic sales queen because you are showing up with a confidence and power your audience has never seen before. More people are moved by your message. More people buy your offers. More people connect to you because you are being authentically you—without any masks, like my client Eloise, a Money Alchemy Coach who worked less than ever but received sales every day and her first £10,000 month.

Family Relationships

The dynamics with your parents, siblings and children dramatically shift as the impact of this work heals intergenerationally like nothing I have seen before. My client Donna, a couples' healer based in Australia, was able to reconnect with her adult children on an even deeper level and heal her relationship with her father—completely lifechanging and so amazing for the generations to follow.

Romantic Relationships

This work has saved marriages, manifested soulmates and improved sex lives. My client Danielle found her passion for her business again, earned $18,000 in sales in thirty-six hours, and had multiple men messaging her to go on a date—one of whom ended up being her soulmate. She directly attributed this to healing her Outcast. We literally made it rain money and men!

Spiritual and Intuitive Gifts

Your hidden spiritual gifts get unlocked. This is probably one of my favourite ever shifts. Even women who think they have none of these skills end up unlocking powerful spiritual and intuitive gifts and getting even better results with their clients. You start to channel ideas for your business that are successful every time. You start to co-create with the universe for bigger impact and success. It's one of my favourite and most important success shifts my clients comment on. Some clients have even gone on to uncover their million-dollar ideas and created their million-dollar bodies of work as a direct result of this. My client Traci, a jeweller from Australia, unlocked powerful intuitive and spiritual gifts, rebranding her whole business to creating channelled priestess jewellery and adding healing sessions to her services. She now teaches others to channel, too!

Business Success and Client Results

This is all about relationships. Everything improves: clients, mentors, your team; your own talents, abilities and gifts skyrocket. Your energy is so different this positively impacts your clients, too, and you attract better clients who get better results. You are able to take your clients deeper because you understand them better due to your own level of healing. Many clients say the power of their own work explodes after working with me, like my client Priyanka, who not only received a £20,000 bonus out of the blue, but realised she was a powerful healer herself, too.

And, because you become an expert in self-sabotage after doing the work yourself, you see the ways *your clients* are sabotaging themselves and, with the knowledge and wisdom you have gained, can help them through.

Health and Wellbeing

Many of my clients are often sabotaging themselves through poor nutrition, struggles with food, lack of exercise or self-neglect without even realising it. In these instances, healing the Success Saboteurs has a huge impact on health and wellbeing. Stubborn weight drops off, burnout and autoimmune symptoms can alleviate or disappear, and your relationship with food and your body can change. After healing her Hustler Success Saboteur, Schadia sold her highest ever priced offers with ease and dropped 17lbs after seven years of struggling with weight and health – even though we didn't do a single thing specifically focused on weight.

How are multidimensional results like this possible? The reason is the one common denominator at the centre of all of those things: *you*!

When we transform you, we transform *everything*.

Figure 3: The Wheel of Results

Everything is a mirror. The jaw-dropping money results are just a side effect of transforming *you* and your relationship with yourself. You will have changed how you feel about yourself and what you believe you are worthy, deserving, and capable of receiving (and holding).

Of course, you will also have a business strategy, but any strategy is only as powerful as the person using it. And often, our Success Saboteur Archetypes are making us dramatically overcomplicate the strategy.

You might have noticed by now that I mix psychology and spirituality in my techniques. But, while I admit to being a little 'woo', my methods are based in logic, too. If you are healing the very things stopping you receiving and holding your next six figures, your next six figures will naturally happen with more ease as a side effect.

Does It Work?

Throughout this book, I will share with you real-life six-figure transformation stories that provide the evidence of what is possible for you; women who have already had their six-figure year, six-figure launches and six-figure months. Women just like my client Dimple, who came to me with inconsistent five-figure months. She had already created a degree of success in her life, but as an ambitious woman, she wanted more. As she began healing her Success Saboteur Archetypes and the wounds underneath them, she made more money in months than she had in the entire previous year. Within just fifteen months, she went from a six-figure business to a seven-figure business!

How did her earnings skyrocket so fast? Because her confidence in herself and her own skills skyrocketed after she healed her Success Saboteur Archetypes. She raised her prices and has been able to keep more of the money she makes and build wealth.

With a combination of one-to-one and group work, we healed the root of her Success Saboteur Archetypes using my five-level Success Imprinting approach—and with nothing holding her back anymore, her success was exponential. She became the Revolutionary Woman capable of receiving, achieving and holding more.

The most amazing thing wasn't necessarily the money, though, but what she could do with that money: holidays for her family; investing in her health and in her family's future.

Think of what you will achieve once all of your Success Saboteur Archetypes are healed and nothing is holding you back any longer! I will share more on the lessons from Dimple's huge six figure leap in Chapter 9.

I really believe that this work is the missing link when it comes to more business success for women. Strategy is not enough. If your Success Saboteur Archetypes are holding you back from acting on those strategies, you will continuously hold yourself back from your full potential.

My big passion behind what I do is to create a world where there are more women impacting the world and being greatly financially rewarded for it. More women who feel safe to do things differently and be the Legacy Maker in their family and in the world.

I have seen time and time again that the inner transformation and the results that come with that lead to women having more choice and more freedom; freedom to live a life that is for them, and freedom to remove themselves from any situation that might not be good for themselves and their children; freedom to break free from the limiting legacies of the generations before us and write new, empowering ones.

I truly believe that when women heal, we heal the world. I believe in a safer, richer world for all women and children, and that is accomplished by empowering them, financially, emotionally and spiritually.

Let's dive deep into the Success Saboteur Archetypes one by one as I take you through my legendary Unconscious Unveiling process to help you see the patterns your next six figures are hiding behind.

3

THE OVERPROTECTOR SUCCESS SABOTEUR ARCHETYPE

This chapter is all about the Overprotector Success Saboteur Archetype. Here, I will unveil what it is, show you how it is blocking you from receiving your next six figures, and, most importantly, how to start healing it so it no longer gets in the way of the unbelievable success you are destined for.

Until summer 2023, I had only identified four Success Saboteur Archetypes. Three and a half years after outlining my theory about the Success Saboteurs, however, I discovered a new one that was impacting me (we all have our blind spots—even me!), and looking back now, it's so obvious that it was there all along. I had been integrating it into all the other Success Saboteurs, so I hadn't *entirely* missed it, but it still needed a name and attention in its own right. I believe this is to be a Master Success

Saboteur—the one that, when healed, acts as a catalyst for the healing of all the others, too.

Here, we will go deep into how this Success Saboteur is keeping you stuck, going around in circles, hiding your true potential, and only ever earning 'safe money' in your business. Your next six-figure leap is currently hiding behind your comfort zone, thanks to this Success Saboteur Archetype. So, it's time to embrace extraordinary levels of success and an overflow of money. Using my investigative mind and experience in uncovering and healing Success Saboteurs in thousands of women, I am going to help you understand where this comes from cognitively so you can start to release it. Grab your notebook and pen and prepare to be mindblown!

Overview of the Overprotector

If you have a strong Overprotector Success Saboteur, you consciously crave more success, but feel, deep down, that it is not safe in some way. You probably felt unsafe many times during your childhood (in your home or school or both), and this fear of success keeps you stuck, going around in circles and doing the same thing over and over again, expecting a different result. It stops you from taking the risks and action needed to create more success.

The Overprotector creates deep blocks around how you perceive success and whether you're safe enough to be more successful than others around you, whether family, friends, mentors, or partners, and so on. I think of the Overprotector Success Saboteur as your inner overprotective mother. She has the best intentions—she wants to protect you from harm, pain, unhappiness, negative experiences, rejection, failure, and disappointments—but she goes a bit too far and keeps you stuck in your comfort zone, or 'safe' zone, only ever allowing you to make 'safe' money and achieve 'safe' success.

Overprotection can be stifling and disempowering. Growth doesn't happen in your comfort zone.

The Overprotector can be quite controlling and restrictive and cause unnecessary anxiety. It is harmful to your growth, and can have negative impacts on your confidence and resilience (which are essential qualities for a successful leader at any level). If you don't heal this Success Saboteur, it will continue to keep you stuck in survival mode, dimming your natural success potential, plateauing in a business that doesn't fulfil you and making leaps you cannot sustain.

Two key ways in which the Overprotector manifests in our lives are:

1. It stops us from taking the risks and actions we need to take in order to become more successful. We feel stuck, we plateau, and we remain in survival mode, because deep down, success doesn't feel safe.
2. It is triggered when we have already grown to a significant level of success. From this point, we will fear making changes, become overcautious, and make decisions more slowly. Your business may plateau or go backwards, and this also triggers survival mode and the belief *more* success is not safe.

The main driver behind the Overprotector is avoiding feeling unsafe. It is the key Success Saboteur in affecting how much success you can hold. If a certain level of success or money feels unsafe in any way, you will stop yourself from having it, or sabotage it if you do get it.

Common Overprotector Beliefs and Feelings

I am going to share the most common beliefs and feelings that indicate you have an Overprotector Success Saboteur holding you back from your next six figures. As you are reading them, ask yourself, 'Does this feel right or wrong for me?' and highlight or make a note of any of the ones that resonate for you.

- 'Success is unsafe/dangerous.'
- 'If I am more successful than others, they will be jealous of me.'
- 'I need to protect myself.'
- 'I am not allowed to outshine my mother/siblings/friends, etc.'
- 'Staying where I am keeps me safe.'
- 'Change scares me.'
- 'Something bad might happen to me if I have more than what I have now.'
- Fear of fucking it up and losing it all.
- Fear of success and how big something could be (this makes you feel frozen).
- Feeling reassured and safe when there is routine, rules, and familiarity.
- Feeling that there have been times where success brought a lot of

pain/confusion.

- Feeling that a certain amount of success and/or money is 'safe', but that any more than that isn't.
- Feeling especially worried about other women's views and reactions to your success.
- Feeling like you aren't 'allowed' to be more successful than others close to you, such as your mother, siblings, friends, peers, or mentors.
- Feeling scared to take risks and change something mediocre for something better.

After noting the ones that resonate with you, you may want to reflect on any other ways this Success Saboteur shows up in your beliefs and feelings and make a note of those too.

How the Overprotector Shows Up at All Levels

There are common ways the Overprotector shows up generally, whatever stage of your six-figure journey you are in right now. Again, just highlight or note down the ones that resonate for you as you are reading through.

- Anxiety or high-functioning anxiety.
- Low moods/depression.
- Not taking action on the activities you know will lead to more success as a way to keep your success limited or 'average'.
- Feeling that a certain figure in your bank account is 'safe'. Anxiety

follows if your balance dips above or below it.

- Going around in circles with business decisions, with huge amounts of avoidance and procrastination.
- Coasting along in your comfort zone doing the same things you have always done, *or* you stop doing the things you know actually work.
- Fear of change (which keeps you stuck or going backwards in your business).
- Dressing down/less glamorously so others don't feel threatened by you.
- Staying in relationships (personal or business) for safety reasons even if they are not healthy or fulfilling.
- Blaming yourself for other people's blocks, bad behaviour, and reactions.
- Overconsuming alcohol or food, and/or alcohol/food addiction (as a way of self-soothing).
- Weight plateaus or holding onto or using weight as a 'shield'.
- Hoarding.
- Liking to keep things the 'same', through eating the same foods regularly, wearing the same clothes a lot, etc.
- Finding you are overprotective of your children or loved ones (to an extreme).
- Constantly playing down or hiding your successes for fear of upsetting others.
- Giving your money away or letting people take advantage of you financially, because you feel guilty about having more than them.
- Lots of people owing you money or services that haven't been

delivered.

- You have no contracts, terms and conditions, or policies in place to protect you or your business.

Now, let's look specifically at how the Overprotector blocks you from that six-figure year, launch, or month. Pay attention to all the different levels discussed, as the symptoms can be fluid across them, and even though you are not there yet, you may notice something that resonates with you (or identify something to look out for!).

How the Overprotector Blocks Your Six-Figure Year

At the zero- to six-figure level in business, the Overprotector mainly manifests in the form of struggles to feel 'safe to be successful' as an entrepreneur rather than as an employee.

You may still be an employee yourself or have recently broken away from that identity by going all in on building your business. Most people you know are employees, and you are already breaking the mould by trying to do something different; to be successful in a different way to how everyone else you are close to is. Your biggest fears surround the reactions of immediate family, friends, and partners around your business and how much money or success you create. Your fears of their reactions are given more importance than your own desires for more success and money.

This leads you to wonder things like:

'Can I have a six-figure business and still be loved and accepted by others?'

'Will my partner feel emasculated by me?'

'Will my friends reject and bitch about me?'

'Will my mother disown or punish me?'

Here are some more specific ways it commonly shows up at this level now. Highlight or note down any that resonate for you:

- Avoiding the biggest needle movers that will actually make you more money, especially if they feel 'too easy'.
- Not completing the things that will bring you more success (e.g., that sales page for that new offer, or that course people have been asking you for).
- Being so worried about what others will think of your success, or that others will somehow feel bad about themselves if you are more successful than them, that you stop yourself from receiving it.
- Not talking enough about your offers or owning how good you are (meaning people end up not seeing the evidence they need in order to buy from you).
- Spending a lot of money on things to improve your success, but never using or taking action on them.
- Not seeming to be able to get past a few thousand dollars a month in revenue.
- Feeling anxious or low when you receive more success, thus leading to the avoidance or sabotage of the things that led to it.
- Having creative blocks (because you are in survival mode and cannot think clearly). This includes struggles to create offers or write marketing content. (This can sometimes be confused for the

Imposter Success Saboteur, which we will get into later.)

- Blaming yourself for a traumatic experience and feeling too frozen to take action against it.
- Feeling too scared to leave your job and go all in on your business.
- Fearing friends turning on you or leaving you out because now you're 'different' to them.
- Intentionally trying to slow your success down if it's 'happening too fast'.
- Being fearful of what your mother/father will say/think/feel if you are more financially successful than them.
- Playing down your ambitions and (surprise, surprise!) them not materialising.
- Avoiding the guilt that comes with having more than the people close to you.
- Fearing that others will try to take your success and money from you and you will struggle to say no.

How the Overprotector Blocks Your Six-Figure Launch

Generally, at the six-figure launch level, you have shifted those earlier fears and have expanded your capacity for success—that is, how much success feels 'safe' to you. You desire more success, but you still don't feel safe enough to have more success in business, especially if you achieve this in a short period of time. You fear whether more success will impact your health and cause burnout. You fear the prospect that you will fuck it up and not be able to hold it all or let clients down, or lose those you love because you are now 'too different', or because they have become jealous and triggered by your growth.

Here are some more specific ways in which the Overprotector manifests at this level:

- You don't feel safe enough to receive and hold onto that much money in one launch. *What bad thing will happen in exchange?*
- You withdraw from or stop your launch before it reaches the target, even though everything is going well.
- You fear what others will think of you if you have 'that much' money so easily within one launch—something so many women aim to make in a year.
- You feel guilty that you will have more than what you 'need' when others have less.
- You fear that people will want money from you and that you will feel financially responsible for them.
- You start neglecting your health or looks as a form of self-punishment and so you can be 'less of a threat', to compensate for having more success.
- You feel you need to have something fail or go wrong so you can 'prove' to others that you struggle still, just like everyone else.
- You worry your coach or mentor will start to see you as competition or a rival.
- You put up with the wrong hires in your team who cost you income and growth because 'they need the money more than you'.
- You keep doing the same launch strategies that are not working, rather than trying something new and different.

- You may hit a six-figure launch and then retreat and sabotage your income afterwards because you don't feel safe to hold that level of money.
- You experience a business trauma and associate it with that level of success.

There is so much shame associated with going backwards in business, and I have worked with many women who have come to me because their business has started to go backwards after experiencing a business trauma—a bad client, an unexpected tax bill they hadn't prepared for, a public attack from their mentor or coach, legal issues or having to lay staff off. Often, an association has been created between that level of success (and fun) in their business and the business trauma, which means until that business trauma is healed, they will continue to experience a downward spiral due to their Overprotector Success Saboteur.

How the Overprotector Blocks Your Six-Figure Month

At this level, you do not feel that it is safe to be successful at the '2% level'—that is, to hold a level of success that only 2% of female entrepreneurs ever statistically reach. Not only do you worry about being different to your nearest and dearest, but you also worry about being different to 98% of the other female entrepreneurs—a community where, by this point, you now feel like you belong. You know that when you have a six-figure month, people will notice. You will be shining and standing out, and that feels scary AF.

Here are some common ways in which the Overprotector shows up at this level:

- The thought of six-figure months actually scares the fuck out of you, as this much abundance feels really unsafe to receive, let alone hold.
- You do not know whether it will be worth risking a good life for the chance of a great one. Should you stay here where it's safe and 'enough'? Or aim bigger?
- You may experience weight gain as a form of self-protection as your income rises.
- Health issues can also manifest as a form of self-protection (ever remember faking illness to protect you from something at school or at home? Your mind and heart have learned that illness keeps you safe).
- Old childhood traumas around 'feeling unsafe' come to the surface.
- You are scared to take the big, bold risks you need to in order to get to the next level.
- You dim your light and power so others don't feel 'threatened' by you.
- Huge dips in confidence.
- You can't hold onto the money that's coming in, so you feel like it's all for nothing. More money feels like it will just be more hassle and hustle.
- You start to tell yourself that less is safer. You drop your ambitious goals and settle for what feels comfortable.

- You may have had a six-figure month already and experienced something that rocked your sense of safety so much you haven't been able to reach it again.
- Your income starts to go backwards to what feels 'safer' to you again.

Where the Overprotector Comes From

You weren't born with an Overprotector Success Saboteur. It developed in response to specific experiences and wounding within relationships you have had. In other words, the Overprotector Success Saboteur is a survival strategy created by your mind when you experience wounding to your sense of safety, especially when that wounding around safety is perceived to be linked to successes. An example of this could be when a child's mother does not protect the child from abuse, or a parent, sibling, or friend never being happy for (or feeling threatened by) the child's successes and instead giving them punishments, criticism and jealousy.

The Overprotector kept us safe in some way as a child, but as an adult, it holds us back. Adult experiences then tend to retrigger this and bring the Overprotector to the surface. I have included some adult experiences here, too.

Here are some more situations that may have led to the development of the Overprotector in your childhood. Read them with an open mind and highlight or note down any that resonate for you:

- A parent that was overly anxious/concerned about your safety.

This may have manifested for them as anxiety, OCD, or them divulging adult information to you, their child, as an attempt to keep you safe.

- A parent that did not protect you, or neglected you.
- A parent/family member/teacher who made you feel unsafe in any way (such as through abuse or singling you out in front of others).
- A female (whether a friend, mother, sister, etc.) who was jealous of your body/intelligence/looks, etc.
- A mother with narcissistic tendencies.
- Being bullied or attacked by other females because you are prettier, slimmer, more intelligent, and/or more successful, or have been given better grades, a promotion, or business success (and so on).
- Being victim blamed or shamed.
- Experiencing or witnessing a huge loss or fall from success (resulting in fear that it could happen again).
- Having to lend money to others (even parents) and it never being paid back.
- Patriarchy (where feminine energy is unsafe to embody or express).
- Bitchiness and backstabbing from other females.
- A parent with a 'poor me' complex that made you feel guilty for having or being more than them.
- Receiving unwanted sexual attention, sexual assault, or sexual abuse.
- Trickery or betrayal from other females.

- Being tricked out of money or something of value.
- Hearing a parent criticise others who are successful.
- An unwritten rule that you weren't allowed to be more successful than your parent or sibling (this is especially common in narcissistic and toxic family dynamics).
- Any form of physical violence or abuse (e.g., mugging; domestic violence; parental).
- A home where rivalry and competition were promoted.
- Experiencing domestic abuse, post-separation abuse, and/or narcissistic abuse.

Where the Overprotector Came from For Me

I shared at the start of this book that I am an abuse survivor. This was chronic abuse that lasted all throughout my childhood and teenage years. Yet, much to my surprise, the biggest part of my healing journey hasn't been from the abuse and the person who inflicted it—it's been healing my heart from the wounds that were created by the people who didn't believe and protect me from that abuse; the people who left me feeling deeply unsafe and unprotected.

So many of my clients experience their deepest healing (and biggest successes) from these *hidden* wounds, too.

When, in adulthood, I started speaking about the abuse I'd endured, refusing to pretend it hadn't happened or to brush it under the carpet, I was victim blamed and shamed.

Let's get one thing straight: no child is *ever* responsible or to blame for the abuse an adult inflicts on them. Ever. The bottom line is, my little self couldn't rely on anything or anyone outside of me to protect me. For much of that traumatic time of my life, protection wasn't available to me, so my poor but clever heart and mind created my inner Overprotector to try to help me stay safe. As a result, I went from being a naturally slim child to a child who piled on over three stone in weight in one summer, developed a food addiction and, ultimately, endured a twenty-year battle with her body. If I was too slim, I felt I'd make women jealous and get unwanted sexual attention from men. If I was too big, I'd be deeply unhappy and uncomfortable in my own body.

I had many experiences that led me to believe that if another woman perceived me to be better or more than her in some way, I'd be in danger—and I learned from a young age that in such a situation, I would be blamed, not protected. Whether it was the mother I felt I couldn't be slimmer or more successful than, the best friend who was jealous when I lost weight and started getting attention from men, or the older landlady (and friend) who would try to compete with me around men, our cooking skills and fitness abilities, every little success I had seemed to trigger the women around me. Then there were the best friends who tricked me out of money or betrayed me by sabotaging my relationships or business.

I don't hold any grudges towards any of these people—I know they were operating from their own wounds at the time—but that doesn't mean my Overprotector Success Saboteur wasn't activated as a result.

My Six-Figure Year

I first started my health food business back in 2014. I naturally fell into it as a way of making some extra money as a social work master's student. The women around me that I was friends with at the time came across as weirdly jealous that I was making a few hundred pounds selling granola and cakes to others at our local CrossFit gym. They even actively promoted the competition, all the while never doing anything to support my little business. This hurt and triggered my old wounds, and taught me that people are jealous of anyone who merely has a business, no matter how successful it is (so you may as well be wildly successful anyway, right?).

Over time, I noticed that close friends never asked how my business was going, and the most supportive people who celebrated every success with me were just acquaintances—never the women close to me.

My 'safe money' was around £33,000 a year (around $40,000), and this was the total I earned from my wage as a social worker and my revenue in my business for the first three years of my business. I coasted at what felt like a safe, 'average' level in my business for a while. I already made more money than anyone I knew, and any more didn't feel safe.

I started to get more and more into self-development and until that point had no idea that fears of success even existed, but it was like a lightbulb turned on when I realised. I was reading Barbara Stanny's *Sacred Success*, in which she had written some journaling prompts that brought my hidden beliefs to light. I had always thought I feared failure, not success!

I held onto my social work job for 'safety' for a while, even though I knew my soul's purpose was my business. It took becoming a single mother with postnatal depression for me to finally go all in on my business and set the goal for a six-figure year. When I made this decision, I had to do lots of inner safety work around leaving my job behind and fully stepping into my identity as 'Natasha the Entrepreneur'; I held onto 'Natasha the Social Worker' for years afterwards before finally letting go of my license to practice. The deep healing around the Overprotector finally allowed my business to explode to its first six figures.

My Six-Figure Launch

I had a traumatic experience with a woman I had invested in, just after my first six-figure sales month. It seemed like one minute, I was being celebrated as a success story, and the next, I was being treated as the competition. It reminded me of a toxic family dynamic where I was the scapegoat—and there was no way I was going back to that kind of life. It brought a lot of old trauma to the surface. Sadly, it's very common to get subconsciously drawn to the dynamics that were normal for you as a child, and we don't always see it until it is too late.

The whole thing left me with anxiety attacks for the first time in my life. I felt deeply unsafe in the world again, and I had to involve solicitors to protect me.

As painful as this whole situation was, it revealed that I had shaky internal foundations (and external ones, too), and this realisation set me on a path to finding safety within again.

There was a problem, though: I now associated that level of success with danger, and so I couldn't sustain it. So, my income dropped massively, falling to $20,000 months again at the start of 2020.

Around that time, my Success Saboteur Archetypes came to me in a dream, but I was too frozen in fear to act on them. Yet I knew deep down that they were going to be incredibly successful. Throughout my entrepreneurial journey, I have noticed that the things I most resist are the things that will most explode my success, and my signature body of work that you are reading about here in this book... boy, did I resist it! I am usually such a fast action taker, but I procrastinated over this for *months*—six, in fact!—before I finally released my Success Saboteur Archetypes Assessment to the world in the summer of 2020.

People went crazy for it! They were begging me for the next steps, even though I had nothing to offer at the time. And that's how my Ultimate Uplevel Academy and signature body of work was born. I procrastinated like crazy (just like I did with this book)—until I didn't, and then my business exploded.

That's the Overprotector Success Saboteur at play!

Birthing a new body of work is literally like birthing a baby: it can be painful, but the end result is worth it. And I am so glad I birthed this baby into the world. In fact, I had *two* six-figure launches, each for a different program at the same time, in the summer of 2020—which is unheard of. Holy quantum leap! When you make big bold moves, the Universe meets you at that level.

My Six-Figure Month

My two six-figure launches were actually the start of my consistent six- (and multi-six-) figure months, too! That deep work I had done on my Overprotector Success Saboteur (even though I didn't realize that's what it was at the time) massively skyrocketed how much success I felt safe enough to hold, and accordingly, my income started to explode—consistently. In March of 2020, I'd been having $20,000 months. By the end of 2020, I was making consistent six-figure months, and 2020 was my first million-dollar year.

Let this be your evidence that anything can happen when you do the work!

I have also had multi-six-figure months, and each new level of success has needed a new level of internal safety; an internal expansion of what feels safe to hold.

My success grew very quick—I was a cash millionaire by the age of thirty-three—and being from such a small town, I didn't know anyone else around me who had achieved that as young as me. Let alone another woman.

In May 2021, I had my first six-figure sales day and a $500,000 sales month. I felt on top of my game. I was feeling healthier and more confident in my body than ever after consistently exercising and taking care of my body again post having my little Oscar. My partner and I were feeling closer than ever. Everything was going amazing in my life. Then, a series of unfortunate events (*cough* sabotage) happened:

1. During the launch itself, multiple people informed me that my

method was being taught in someone else's certification (they'd recognised my work in the launch event).

2. Not long after that, I felt publicly attacked online after my words around a new offer were misinterpreted by someone who was a previous mentor and peer of mine. I stopped working on this book's manuscript that very same day.
3. I broke my arm in a freak accident while partying on Richard Branson's island (after marrying my soulmate on that island under the full moon that same evening).
4. I was dealing with a personal battle that was hugely linked to safety.
5. There was a huge disruption within my team, including a sudden resignation mid-launch (impeccable timing!).
6. A friend who was working as a contractor in my business suddenly told me she was jealous of how much money my clients pay me and stopped fulfilling the work she had been paid for.

As you can see, it wasn't one bad thing that happened; it was a collection of things. And every time one more thing happened, I was never sure whether it would be the straw to break the camel's back, so to speak. I remember thinking at one point, *If this is success, I don't want it.* My internal relationship with success started to change. I decided, 'Everything was much safer when I was only making six figures a month. Any more than that is dangerous.' I stopped taking care of myself and I gained weight. I worked on all the other Success Saboteurs (especially the Outcast and Imposter), not realising it was a different one entirely. Things started to grow again. Then came the summer, and I had this deep intuitive feeling I was going to have a $500,000 launch of my HeartHealing Mastery Certification. When the launch easily reached $350,000 and my intuition looked like it was becoming reality, I completely stopped the launch. I had already associated $500,000 as being unsafe, due to the series of unfortunate events that had unfolded after the $500,000 month I'd had the year before.

Unbeknownst to me, that final experience around a jealous friend and money retriggered a whole pattern linked to feminine wounding that led right back to my mother wound. This was my 'original' feminine wound—the one where I didn't feel safe to be 'more than' other women; where fears of jealousy, competition and rivalry had really stemmed from.

Clearly, I was going around in circles. I had never pulled the plug on a launch before, least of all one that was going so well. My revenue went backwards, too—not much, but enough to show me that something wasn't right here. I missed my original book launch date entirely because I couldn't bring myself to open the manuscript and finish it. I was still showing up in my business, but it was as if my shine and confidence had been dulled. Things just weren't working in the same way anymore.

Then, one day, I dreamt about this new Success Saboteur—the Overprotector—and woke up with it in my mind. It finally clicked: I had gone through all of this so I could understand, on a personal level, how important this Success Saboteur is and the fact that I had to bring it into my work with other women.

And so the Overprotector Success Saboteur was born!

As usual, I used myself as the guinea pig and since healing it myself, all my personal limits around success are gone. All the circles I was going around in, procrastinating on the things that would bring me the most success (including this book!), stopped. I stopped caring about other women being jealous and decided that my mission is too big to let jealousy stop me. They can be jealous of me, or they can join me; that's their choice and responsibility, not mine. Not only do I feel safe enough to be successful around other women, but I ensure I am a safe person to myself. I take care of myself more—I released the extra 'safety weight' I was holding onto—with ease. I have absolute unwavering confidence that, in a few years' time, I'll be sharing insights from my next huge levels of growth again.

When I look back on all my biggest leaps in my career so far, I realised that, just like before I had my first six-figure launch, I did deep work on the Overprotector throughout my whole journey; I just hadn't realised how key it was, or that it was a separate Success Saboteur to work on in its own right.

How the Overprotector Looks When It Is Healed

When we heal our Overprotector Success Saboteur, we are finally able to feel safe in our success, no matter what others say or do or how they react to it. We know these responses from other people are not about us, and that our success does not take away from anyone else's; their journey will just go on how it was meant to. We can feel safe enough to receive and hold higher levels of success in all areas of our lives.

Here are some specific ways in which a healed Overprotector may manifest in your life:

- The belief, 'It's safe for me to be feminine, powerful, and successful, and to have a lot of money.'
- You feel safe enough to receive and hold higher levels of success in multiple areas of your life (not just your business).
- You shift from making 'safe' money to making 'unbelievable' money.
- You take powerful, fast, decisive action that drives your business forward every day.
- You create safety and support in every area of your life.
- You ignite your creative spark.
- You release weight or experience freedom from health issues that you have been using as 'protection'.
- You stand in your power as a successful woman, knowing that people will love you for you.
- You stand in your power when you experience business or personal traumas, with the knowledge that you can protect yourself.
- You feel safe enough to take the risks you need to take in order to grow your six- or seven-figure empire.
- You ten times the standards for your life, relationships, and business.
- You have the resilience to weather all of the normal ups and downs of business like a true empress. Nothing fazes you. Nothing triggers you. You don't see threats where you may have before. You buckle in and stand in your power, no matter what.

Gifts Behind the Overprotector

The biggest gift that lies behind the healing of the Overprotector is the Gift of Limitless Success. You are naturally an incredibly successful person, destined for huge things. Success is your middle name, and now, it's time to embrace that instead of hiding from it. Nobody benefits from you playing small: not you; not your family; not your clients. You have a natural 'success essence' that you get to share with the right people. Nobody else gets to take it from you. When you feel safe in your success, your potential is limitless.

For too long, women have been denied their birthright around success, riches, and wealth. For too long, women have tried to create success the way men have said they should, forgetting their feminine power in the process and instead operating too far into the masculine and fighting against their natural 'success essence'. You have been taught to fear the feminine because this is what kept you subordinate to men. We become more powerful when we feel safe to access and combine our feminine energy with the masculine energy that has got us to this point of our success journey.

Stop rejecting the most powerful part of you. Create success *your* way.

Other gifts that you unlock when you heal the Overprotector are:

Figure 4: The Overprotector Success Saboteur

It's safe for you to be successful and powerful.

Healing the Overprotector

You should now clearly see how the Overprotector Success Saboteur is showing up in your money, relationships, and business.

On a scale of one to ten (with ten being the most), rate how much the Overprotector is blocking you from receiving your next six figures.

The time we have spent in this chapter exploring the Overprotector Success Saboteur will already have created significant shifts for you, and I can imagine you are already feeling amazed by the insights you have had. Now you can see why the women who choose to work with me more closely to heal their Success Saboteurs in my Ultimate Uplevel Academy get such incredible results.

Let's take the healing of the Overprotector a little deeper now using my Success Imprinting: Five Levels of Healing approach.

Mind Healing

You have already uncovered a lot of the hidden beliefs around your Overprotector in this chapter. Start to rewrite the beliefs you have unveiled at the root of your Overprotector Success Saboteur by finding evidence to prove each one wrong. E.g., For, 'Others will be jealous of my success,' think of a time where others celebrated and were happy for your success. This creates evidence of a different story instead of the limiting ones you have decided are fact.

Heart Healing

Look back at the root causes of the Overprotector Success Saboteur that resonated with you earlier and consider, who was involved in the first time and worst time? This indicates both the key experiences and the key relationships that you would benefit from doing some healing work in relation to (should you wish to release the Overprotector Success Saboteur further). These will mostly be connected to wounds inflicted by women. You can begin this process by writing a therapeutic letter to that person releasing any anger or hurt you feel towards them and taking your power and safety back. Read it out loud as if saying it to them for extra emotional release.

Soul Healing

Write a healing letter to the part of you that first learned she was not safe enough to be successful. Tell her what she needs to hear from you in order to let go of this pattern and feel safe to be her naturally successful self again. Read this letter out loud to yourself, as if you were reading it out to her. Afterwards, visualise yourself hugging her and merging with her as you become one.

Energy Healing

Write a letter to your inner Overprotector. Thank her for her support in trying to help you, and explain that she can relax now; that you've got this. You are ready for more success, and you are not afraid anymore. Ask her to become something else instead—something that will help you to receive, achieve and hold your next six figures with ease.

Action Healing

Look back at all the ways in which you have identified the Overprotector to be manifesting for you. Write out the following sentence and complete it, multiple times, until nothing new comes out:

One thing I can do to start breaking my Overprotector pattern is […].

This can be one tiny action, the first step. Then, go and do as many of those tiny actions as possible.

Want to go bigger? Often, our goals feel scary because we literally haven't thought any bigger than them. Think way bigger—and take action towards it. Imagine you 10x'd your financial or success goal. What would that look like? Describe it in detail. What would you need to do differently to achieve and receive the 10x version of your success? How can you start taking action on this *now*?

4

THE OVERGIVER SUCCESS SABOTEUR ARCHETYPE

Let's talk about how the Overgiver Success Saboteur is blocking you from receiving your next six figures in your business.

When I was writing this chapter, it was quite painful for me to acknowledge some of my past overgiving behaviours—but what's really important to acknowledge here is that the Overgiver Success Saboteur is not your fault (even if it is your responsibility to heal it). These are patterns that have developed because of what you have been through in your childhood. As a child, you were completely innocent and therefore couldn't be expected to shape your behaviour with the knowledge, foresight and hindsight of that of an adult, so once again, leave any guilt or shame right here. What's most important is that now you have the chance to change this.

Also, I am not a finished product. We are never a finished product. We are human beings who are continuously healing and evolving ourselves. Healing is not a 'one and done' game. We are not something that is broken that needs to be fixed. We are all on a journey of continuous healing.

Part of this process includes being able to recognise the patterns of the Success Saboteurs in yourself so that you can experience breakthroughs, grow and transform, and release yourself from these behaviours.

I will unveil exactly how the Overgiver Success Saboteur is showing up in your mind, money, marketing, and sales—and even in your relationships! Once you understand this, you will be able to heal it so your next six figures can be received quickly and with more ease. You will never charge enough, have enough, or feel enough until you heal the Overgiver Success Saboteur.

Overview of the Overgiver Saboteur

The Overgiver Success Saboteur is the strongest and most common Success Saboteur among female entrepreneurs. You might *think* it's not affecting your behaviour or decisions, but you will probably be surprised by the sneaky ways in which it can do so. Using the insights I have gained from my experience in uncovering and healing the Overgiver Success Saboteur in myself and thousands of women, I am going to help you to understand where this comes on a cognitive level, and I will show you the patterns and hidden ways in which it shows up so that you can start to release your overgiving patterns. These patterns are blind spots you form beneath an unhealed Overgiver Success Saboteur, and these blind spots are blocking your next six-figure year, launch, or month.

There are two key ways in which this particular archetype shows up. You might resonate with one or both. Either way, we all have this archetype in us.

1. Overgiving to everyone, at your own expense. You are stuck in a cycle of people pleasing, you struggle to say no, and/or you are undercharging (or working for free!). You want to 'rescue' and save others. You may have a deep desire to take care of others and go above and beyond for them (and even rescue them), whether clients, family, or friends. Helping and giving to others feels like your life's calling. Whilst this is an admirable quality to have, you often end up sacrificing yourself in some way, and you struggle to say no even when something adds extra stress and strain to you. This can lead to underlying resentment or feelings of being taken advantage of.
2. Overgiving, discounting, and undercharging to those you have an emotional connection with—so you can 'stay safe'. This is called 'fawning', and fawning is known as the 'fourth trauma response'—a term coined by author and psychotherapist Pete Walker. If you felt unsafe in childhood with someone you were emotionally close to, you learned to 'people please' as a way to stay safe. This shows up particularly with relatives, loved ones, friends, favourite clients or long-term clients.

This desire to rescue others, associated with the Overgiver, often comes from deep down wishing someone had done that for you. But it is coming from the wrong energy, because rescuing people often disempowers them (the opposite of what we are often trying to achieve!). The only person who can ever really rescue you is you. Through healing our Overgiver, we become our own rescue.

The Overgiver Success Saboteur primarily wants to avoid abandonment or feelings of 'I am not good enough'. It wants to be liked by everyone! It also affects pricing and your capacity to receive abundance. If you don't heal the Overgiver Success Saboteur, you will continue to overgive, and this will limit your capacity to receive, it will keep you stuck, and it will keep you undercharging and depleting yourself. You may even develop resentment towards your business, clients, or even your team. While the Overprotector (which we explored in the previous chapter) manifests as you 'overmothering' yourself, the Overgiver is when you 'overmother' *others* and put them before yourself.

Common Overgiver Beliefs and Feelings

I am going to share the most common beliefs and feelings that indicate you have an Overgiver Success Saboteur holding you back from your next six figures. As you are reading them, just ask yourself, 'Does this feel right or wrong for me?' and highlight or make a note of any of the ones that resonate for you.

After noting the ones that resonate with you, you may want to reflect on any other ways this Success Saboteur shows up in your beliefs and feelings and make a note of those too.

- 'I am not lovable for who I really am.'
- 'I must please others in order to be loved/liked/accepted.'
- 'I am not enough.'
- 'It is not safe for me to be myself.'
- 'People need me to rescue/save them.'
- 'Putting others' needs before mine makes me a good person.'
- 'It's selfish to put myself first.'
- 'Others are more important than me.'
- 'My needs and wants are not important.'
- 'Helping others is more important than making money.'
- Feeling taken advantage of and resentful but unable to express it.
- Feeling not good enough/smart enough/attractive enough/successful enough.
- Feeling you are not allowed to have needs or express your own needs as they are not important or less important than others'.
- Worrying about people abandoning you or not liking you if you do not overgive to them.
- Feeling most worthy when helping/rescuing others.
- Feeling safe when keeping others happy to avoid conflict.

Some of these beliefs and feelings are deeply ingrained in us from childhood—particularly in cultural and gendered expectations of what it is to be a woman.

Well, not in my world! We are Revolutionary Women. We are redefining what it means to be a woman in this world, and we are showing our children and future generations that it gets to be different.

As a modern-day champion for women and a mum to two boys, I

caught myself feeling disappointed that I didn't also have a daughter to break the mould for. But then I realised, I get to raise my boys into healed men who see and treat women differently! I realised how powerful that is, and how needed it is in the world.

We often get stuck in the thinking that helping others is the most important thing, but I believe that you can help others *and* make money. I am all about serving others, but making money is equally important. You deserve to be rich as a result of the impact and help you put out into the world.

When you believe that helping others is more important than making money, you always sacrifice yourself and your income to help others and remain poor at the end of the month, no matter how much money you make. That is not a healthy approach to business. That leads to burnout, and it leads to you not having enough for you and your family.

How the Overgiver Shows Up at All Levels

There are common ways the Overgiver shows up generally, whatever stage of your six-figure journey you are in right now. Again, just highlight or note down the ones that resonate for you as you are reading through.

- You have huge difficulties around boundaries, personally, professionally, physically, and emotionally.
- You have patterns around or fear of money, and worry about success abandoning you. You imagine that you will 'lose it all' one day, so you reason that it is easier to not have it than to have it and

experience the pain of losing it.

- You have phases of Restricted Receiving where you can't seem to receive much more than what you *need*. You might find you are stuck just scraping by, with just enough to cover your bills every month, even if you make a lot of money. Restricted Receiving can occur at any level of success (even the six-figure month level!).
- You have deep fears of clients leaving you (because your abandonment wound still runs deep), so you overgive to keep them around.
- You take it personally when your clients don't commit, when they quit, or when they don't get results. You blame yourself, believing it's your responsibility to deliver the transformation, even though, logically, you know you gave them everything they needed in order to be successful and that they simply didn't participate in the co-creation.
- You are massively triggered by others having healthy boundaries, because deep down, you wish you could do this for yourself. Their boundaries highlight your own lack of boundaries.
- You do everything to be a perfect partner, including showering them with gifts and going above and beyond, and feeling resentful when you don't get the same back. (This is because you are overgiving just to get something back, not to serve/help others.)
- Any sexual pleasure seeming to be one-sided and more about them than you. (When we overgive, we give people permission to overtake.)
- You drop everything to see your partner when *they* want to and

to see to your clients when they 'need' you.

- You do everything for your partner/mother/friends/clients.
- You don't pay yourself first (or at all).
- You never celebrate big successes, spend only what you *need* to (not what you *desire* to), and/or only ever treat others.
- You have health, financial, or relationship issues.
- You blame your coach or mentor when you don't get results, slipping into a victim mindset.
- You believe you need a coach all the time in order to be successful, in a codependent way. This is different energy from a desire to have a coach who expands you; rather, you feel that you won't ever be successful without one.
- You feel guilty if you start to earn more than your partner.
- You get stuck in toxic client or mentor dynamics, and don't identify them as such until you're out of them.
- You find it hard to uphold contracts or follow up on missed payments.

This is a long list of the most common ways in which the Overgiver Success Saboteur blocks your progress, but it isn't an exhaustive one; there are still more. I am now going to take you through more specific ways it shows up to block your six-figure year, launch or month.

How the Overgiver Blocks Your Six-Figure Year

At the zero- to six-figure year level, your Overgiver blocks your six-figure year either because you are a) dramatically overgiving to your clients and not charging anywhere near enough to make six figures a reality, and/or b) you are overgiving to your family and friends and not making enough time for your business.

Highlight any of the below common behaviours associated with the Overgiver Success Saboteur that you recognise as blocking *your* six-figure year.

- You don't feel you are good enough to be paid well for what you do, so you often undercharge, do extra work for free, do trades or swaps or don't charge at all.
- You place clients' needs above your own, so will overdeliver at the expense of your health and/or your family/personal time.
- You are always running around doing everything for family and friends, and have no time left for your business.
- You base pricing on what you think others can afford and not on the transformation you provide.
- You try to keep your prices low to people please and fear people abandoning you if your prices are too high.
- You are quick to spend your hard-earned money on others, but not yourself.
- You 'mother' your clients (and possibly your partner, too).
- You offer lifetime support on programs.
- You spend all your income on the next coach/course you believe is going to save you, rather than saving it.
- You offer free coaching 'for testimonials'. (Psst: you will never get the same result from someone who has had a service for free as

from someone who paid for the service!)

- You build a business based on what you think other people want, not what you want to deliver and what you want to bring to your business.
- You write huge advice posts with tons of tips hoping people will like it enough to buy from you, but avoid asking for the sale in case you 'annoy' people.
- Deep down, your desire to be liked is overriding your ability to make money.
- You have difficulties niching down because you are trying to be everything to everyone.
- You say yes to everything and have poor boundaries.
- You attract very wounded and demanding clients.

All these experiences are very normal when your Overgiver is running the show. I really believe everyone in business goes through this at some point in their journey. I, for one, used to have a super-strong Overgiver. It is something that I have to work through at every new level I reach.

If you believe a coach or a course is responsible for saving you and for your results, you also (subconsciously) believe that about your relationship dynamic with your own clients too. That takes personal responsibility away from your clients, and you may find you energetically attract drama triangle situations with clients who think your job is to save them, and will blame you when they don't get the results they wanted.

Healing the Overgiver is about becoming the same type of client you want to attract. When you overgive, you give permission to others to overtake—and when that happens, you will start to feel uncomfortable and resentful, and you will not enjoy your work. Your client is responsible for their results, and you are responsible for delivering to them what they need in order to get the results. It is a beautiful co-creation of your magic and theirs.

Sell more! Selling is serving. When someone buys from you, you are giving them the space to make a commitment to creating a change in their life. If you aren't selling, you are letting your clients down. They need what you have to offer; you have something to offer that they can't get anywhere else. There is no one else out there like you, with your skills and your wisdom, who can deliver what you deliver in the way that you deliver it. You might not believe this about yourself (yet!), but it's true!

How the Overgiver Blocks Your Six-Figure Launch

At the six-figure launch level, there is still some overgiving with clients (although it's getting better!) but the overgiving mostly shifts to overgiving to your team members and in your launch processes.

Here are some more specific ways it commonly shows up at this level. Highlight or note down any that resonate for you:

- You overgive in your launch to the point where you can actually put people off working with you, because you come across as needy. (I caught myself doing this after the birth of my second child!)
- You hire people you are trying to save, or for 'convenience', even though they are not quite the right fit (e.g., family; friends; clients).

- You overgive to your team, making sure that they are all getting paid, bonuses, and extras, while you aren't paying yourself or giving yourself bonuses or gifts.
- You have deep guilt around raising your prices and struggle to say no to people asking for discounts on your signature work.
- You pay for everything when out with friends/family/partner because you feel guilty about how much money you earn.
- You find yourself 'mothering' your team (and still some clients), and find they are not working effectively or taking responsibility for their side of things.
- You struggle to fire people who are not doing their job well enough, or you try to 'performance manage' them out of guilt. You blame yourself for not doing enough for them.
- You add ten different bonuses to your offer, especially if you've increased your prices, because you feel that if you give more than more people will buy (this comes across as needy and puts people off).
- Lots of people saying they can't afford you then investing more somewhere else.
- You are delivering offers that bore you or drain you, because you think it is what your audience want.
- Negative experiences where you have had boundaries with clients you have previously overgiven to and they have reacted badly, triggering your fawn trauma response.
- You already feel burned out by your current launches and are attracting the wrong types of clients who need lots of handholding into your services, so it feels like bigger launches

would equal bigger problems.

My clients often ask, 'What is the difference between overdelivering and overgiving?' Listen, I am a firm believer in overdelivering in business. It has been key to how I've made multi millions with a very small audience and high percentage of return clients. Always overdeliver. For me, the difference is the intention in which it comes from. You see, overgiving isn't actually done from a place of altruism. It is done to meet a need, obtain a result or as an attempt to control the outcome. For example, overgiving to secure a sale or people pleasing a wrong fit client you don't feel safe with versus overdelivering after someone has become a client and is already happy are two very different energies.

Let me give you an example. I always think back to the time I was about to have my C-section with my youngest, Oscar, and was running a launch for my Ultimate Uplevel Academy. In my head, I needed that launch to go well to feel like I could relax after the birth. My energy wasn't in the right place. I had a deep fear of childbirth too that was impacting me. I was thinking about how much 'I' needed the money that would come in from that launch. It was all 'me, me, me' energy, and I began to dramatically overgive. People were messaging me saying, 'I'm in! Send me the signup link,' and I was like, *Oh, yay! Have this too, and this!* and I couldn't figure out why all these people who had said they were signing up then didn't! I realised afterwards I had totally slipped into my Overgiver and it was repelling people like crazy.

How the Overgiver Blocks Your Six-Figure Month

At the six-figure month level, the Overgiver shows up as us not feeling good enough to reach that level of success or as fear and guilt of 'leaving others behind' and not being likable and relatable anymore.

Highlight any of the below common symptoms associated with the Overgiver Success Saboteur that you recognise as blocking *your* six-figure month.

- You have fear and guilt about 'leaving others behind' and please others by staying small.
- You fear that you will not be likable and relatable anymore if you do reach higher income levels.
- You compare yourself to others making six-figure months and feel not good enough.
- You feel a pang of jealousy when your clients don't re-sign or they move onto another coach who charges a lot more than you do.
- Although a lot of money is coming in, you are spending it all back out on others.
- You have reduced your capacity for six-figure month expansion because you are not upholding boundaries with your one-to-one and group clients (e.g., privately supporting clients in group coaching).
- You allow yourself to be accessed at all times by responding to voice notes/ Voxer/emails, even though this is outside of the package the client purchased.
- You feel deep guilt about becoming unaffordable for some, so you

are still undercharging, though the experience and results your clients receive is worth much more.

- You feel resentful that clients do not acknowledge the impact your work had on them.
- You have a need to feel needed, so you stay involved in areas of your business that could be handled by another team member, or things that a client should be doing for themselves.
- Positioning yourself as a 'rescuer' in your brand or marketing (and so attracting people who want to be rescued).
- You struggle to have boundaries when clients copy or steal your work.
- You are already feeling burned out at your current income level and physically cannot serve any more clients the way you are currently serving them.
- A ton of money leaks. There is lots of outstanding debt or long-term debt owed by clients, and they are still accessing services.

Every new level of business that you grow to needs a new level of boundaries; otherwise, the Universe won't deliver it to you—because you haven't got the boundaries in place to be able to hold that next level of clients. Boundaries are an act of love, and boundaries are something you are always working on, just like a new level of a computer game that you have to pass before you can move onto the next one.

Reflect on how the Overgiver Success Saboteur is blocking your next six figures based on everything we have discussed so far.

Where the Overgiver Comes From

Just like with the other Success Saboteurs, you weren't born with an Overgiver Success Saboteur; it is a defence mechanism that developed in response to a specific collection of wounds in your childhood. It is a survival strategy your mind created in response to childhood experiences that made you feel not lovable, not enough, not loved unconditionally, or not safe. It was meant to help us and keep us safe in some way as a child, but as an adult, it holds us back. Uncovering and healing the root cause of the Overgiver Success Saboteur can free us to move forward. Often, this can be a result of the expectations of people around you (especially parents), bullying, or expectations you placed on yourself to be different or perfect so you could be loved or belong. You try to gain love and acceptance through overgiving.

Many things can trigger it. Here are some examples to help you explore where your Overgiver Success Saboteur might have come from. Highlight or note down any that resonate with you.

- Feeling not loved or not good enough.
- Feeling unsafe in school or at home.
- Emotional abandonment (i.e., lack of love or warmth from parent).
- Being loved or praised only when you were doing something for someone else (rather than just being praised for who you are).
- Having perfectionistic/critical parents.
- Being around others who lead with fear.
- Being part of (or witnessing) a scapegoat and golden child

dynamic.

- Not feeling safe enough to say no
- Not feeling safe enough to ask for things.
- Repeated lack of boundaries in the family home.
- Bullying.
- Abuse in the family home (any kind).
- Struggles to fit in at school.
- Abuse outside the family home.
- Parentification.
- Being criticised for your success or mistakes.
- Inconsistent caregiving.
- A narcissistic parent/dysfunctional family.
- A parent who was also a huge Overgiver/codependent.
- Domestic violence relationships.

Reflect on and recognize how these patterns may be showing up in your relationship with money and in your life and business today. When we break these patterns, we start making money with more ease, and our business and relationships are completely transformed.

Where the Overgiver Came from For Me

I am sharing my story with you because stories can help you to have realisations about yourself, too. You may resonate and find awareness for yourself with my situation.

I grew up around many people who led with fear. I didn't have safety, stability, or unconditional love as a child. I felt completely unlovable, and had very few friends. If I did have friends, I would overgive to them to be liked or to be safe with them.

This pattern continued into my adulthood: I learned to please others to stay safe and to overgive to be liked or loved. I would always go above and beyond for friends and partners, doing extravagant things and paying for everything with the little money I had, trying to make them love me. 'Why am I not enough?' was a thought I constantly had when things didn't work out yet again, even though these people never really treated me very well in return.

After the incident where I was almost killed by an ex-partner, I realised that I was looking for love in all the wrong places and that I couldn't go back to the way things were before.

I changed my degree to psychology with criminology and gave my studies my all, and that decision brought me to where I am today.

Things improved for me, but that Overgiver was still there. When I first came into business, I didn't charge enough, tried to serve everyone, had zero boundaries with clients, and got taken advantage of. I also invested in some very wounded coaches and mentors that kept me in a place of fawning and staying small to stay safe.

The more I healed my past and myself, the more I was able to lead myself with love, and the less I found myself in these kinds of relationship dynamics. I was able to put structure and boundaries in place to protect myself, and I was able to spot those types of people better and not get involved in drama triangles. Interestingly, the most healthy love relationship I had (and the man I am married to today) was the one where I was no longer overgiving—because I felt enough just for being me.

My Six-Figure Year

When I was aiming for a six-figure year, I was severely undercharging (including a lifetime-access group program with live support for just £14… Yes, you read that right). My first big lesson in boundaries involved increasing the price for the lifetime-access program. After two years of giving loads of support to and going truly above and beyond for one particular client (who'd paid that £14 fee), I nervously announced that I was releasing new material that would cost an upgrade fee of £30 (about US $35) to access.

She went mad at me and told me I was a 'money grabber'.

This was a very real example of me overgiving and her overtaking. Neither of us ended up happy. She felt I was a money grabber and I felt baffled that I had done so much for this client and she *still* wasn't happy. I eventually started to charge £250 per package for one-to-one work (and was ridiculously overbooked!), and realised that it was physically impossible for me to actually grow a six-figure business at the prices I was charging. Something had to change.

Every time I increased my prices, I was convinced that fewer people would buy—and yet more people bought than ever before.

Whether or not people will buy from you doesn't come down to your pricing (to an extent); it's about what people perceive they will get from what you're offering and making sure you are speaking to the person who sees the value in that price point. If you show someone that you have exactly what they need and show them that you have the confidence to deliver the results, they will make it happen, regardless of the price. I now charge thousands for my signature group program and five figures to work with me one-to-one. I still undercharge compared to other people who deliver the kind of results I do, but it's always a work in progress; a constant evolution. Compared to the past, I have come a long way, and I know you can too.

My Six-Figure Launch

When I started aiming for a six-figure launch, I very quickly realised I didn't have the energetic capacity to hold more clients in my group programs because I didn't have the right pricing or boundaries. This had to shift in order for me to grow. I would see my own wounds in other people and fall into the trap of trying to save or protect that person, so I had to let go of trying to save and 'mother' others so that I could *empower* them (and impact more people in the process). I also found that lots of people were saying they couldn't afford my then-signature program that was £997.

Also, all of my team's time was being taken up with a low-priced membership I was running that had an extortionate amount of admin with just 100 members in it. It wasn't just me that struggled with overgiving—my team did too. We just didn't have strong enough boundaries (it is something I am constantly reassessing personally and within my team).

I decided to close down my signature program and my low-priced membership and launched a higher-priced signature program instead with the aim to get better results. Suddenly, people who had not been able to afford to invest £997 before were paying me double that in full! That new signature program, the Ultimate Uplevel Academy, was my first six-figure launch. This was also the first time I introduced a time boundary with limited access instead of lifetime access as a way of ensuring people did the work and didn't drift for years without committing. I stopped overgiving with memberships that drained me, time and low pricing, and people respected and wanted my work more. My client results and business exploded! My consistent six-figure months began around this same time.

My Six Figure Month

I also had to get comfortable with knowing that not everyone was going to like me, with some clients not liking my boundaries (even though they were loving boundaries that were ultimately there to help them), and with protecting myself and my work.

Every time I uplevelled my prices I felt fear, but rode it out. Every time I uplevelled my income, I noticed something I call 'the shedding'. This is where some clients fall away because they are not meant to grow to that new level with me.

Although it can feel highly triggering for your Overgiver, it's actually a good thing when this happens; it means clients that are more aligned with your new level and new energy can come in. I have the most incredible clients—women who are doing huge things in the world—and I never would have been able to welcome these women into my world without this necessary 'shedding'.

Furthermore, I realised it was logistically impossible for me to serve the amount of people I would need in order to create a seven-figure business at the prices I was still charging, so I upped my prices again and I was quickly overrun with clients!

The universe also sent me tests for my legal boundaries (to see if I had the boundaries I would need for my next level of business, *without* my life crumbling around me), and I passed the test. That was my million-dollar year in my business.

I was ready to receive and hold my next level. I had shown that I had become the woman who had the right boundaries in place, and I was rewarded with my next level.

Very interestingly, a huge shedding happened when I was pregnant with my son, Oscar (my first multi-seven-figure sales year), because any 'mothering' energy I had still been giving to my clients suddenly had to be reserved for my growing baby. Those clients that were subconsciously attracted to my overgiving 'mother' energy (and needed that from me) fell away.

Healing the heart wounds at the root of the Overgiver Success Saboteur was key to changing how I interacted with others in my business. As a result of my healing, I began attracting better and healthier friendships, clients, and family into my life.

How the Overgiver Looks When It Is Healed

When we heal our Overgiver Success Saboteur, we are finally able to lead ourselves with the love we should have received all along and have the boundaries necessary to have the life we want, too. It creates dramatic changes in every area of our life. Specifically:

- You finally feel safe enough to be who you really are.
- You live life for yourself.
- You put healthy boundaries around your relationships and businesses so you get to live a life you love, have time with the people you love, and get to do what you love.
- You charge well for your work and receive higher levels of money, including that next six figures, with so much more ease and joy.
- Your marriage and relationships become healthier and more passionate.
- Your ability to nourish and care for yourself reaches a whole other level.
- You model for others (including your clients and children) what it's like to put yourself first, have healthy boundaries, and have self-love.
- You love selling because you see selling as service, and you *love* receiving money for serving. You know that if you are always overgiving, you are always capping how much you can receive.
- You begin to sell offers that light you up and do what you want to do, which makes more money (because it is more aligned with your soul and life purpose).
- You begin to receive that next six-figures—on repeat!

This is one of my favourite Success Saboteurs to heal: it has led to my clients' marriages being saved and their children's behaviour completely transforming. The women I serve are finally able to put themselves first for the first time in their lives. They are doubling and tripling their prices—sometimes they are even increasing their prices by ten times—and *still* selling out. They begin shifting their business to what lights them up, not what someone else wants them to do. They become magnetic to healthy love and healthy clients.

Gifts Behind the Overgiver

There are incredible gifts hiding behind our Success Saboteurs. Often, our biggest gifts are the very things that others once made us feel bad or not accepted for, or not capable of—so you shut down your gifts and begin to fear them instead.

When you heal the Overgiver, you unlock the Gift of Leadership. You are here to be a powerful leader—someone who influences the world through her ability to lead herself and others with love, compassion and boundaries.

Other gifts that are unlocked when you heal the Overgiver are:

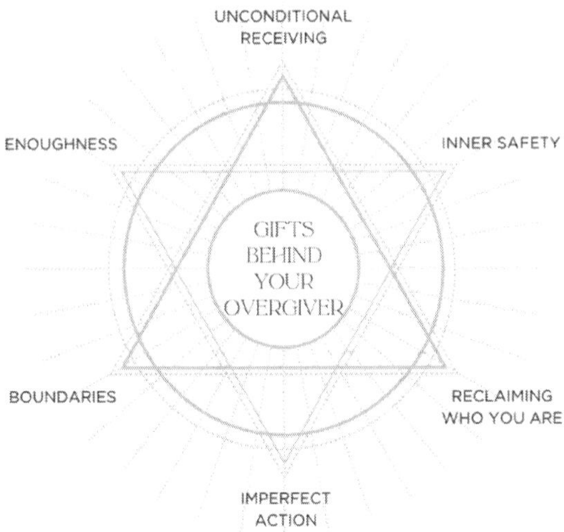

Figure 5: The Overgiver Success Saboteur

Healing the Overgiver

Now that you have read this chapter, you should clearly see how the Overgiver Success Saboteur is showing up in your money, relationships, and business.

On a scale of one to ten (with ten being the most), rate how much the Overgiver is blocking you from receiving your next six figures.

The unveiling process in this chapter will already have created significant shifts for you around this Success Saboteur, but let's take it deeper with some additional healing tasks based on my Success Imprinting approach.

Mind Healing

Start to rewrite the conscious and hidden beliefs you have uncovered at the root of your Overgiver Success Saboteur and find evidence to prove them wrong. You can create your own mini audio of all of the positive opposites that you can play to yourself on repeat whilst doing chores or walking the dog.

Heart Healing

Look back at the root causes of the Overgiver Success Saboteur that resonated with you earlier and consider, who was involved in the first time and worst time? This indicates both the key experiences and the key relationships that you would benefit from doing some healing work around, should you wish to release the Overgiver Success Saboteur further. You can begin this process by writing a therapeutic letter to that person releasing any anger or hurt you feel towards them and taking your power back. Read it out loud as if saying it to them for extra emotional release.

Soul Healing

Write a healing letter to the part of you that first learned she had to please and overgive to others in order to stay safe; the part of you that learned that her needs were not as important as others'. Tell her what she needs to hear from you in order to let go of this pattern and feel safe enough to put herself first again and just be who she really is. Tell her how loved and how enough she is.

Read this letter out loud to yourself, as if you were reading it to her. Afterwards, visualise yourself holding her tight and merging with her as you become one.

Energy Healing

Write a letter to your inner Overgiver. Thank her for all the ways she has supported you and kept you safe, and explain that you would like her to support you in a different way now moving forward. Imagine her merging into a beautiful, queenly part of you who is so ready to receive. Declare out loud all the things you are ready to receive now.

Action Healing

Look back on all the ways in which the Overgiver is showing up for you. Write out the following sentence and complete the sentence again and again, until nothing new comes out:

One thing I can do to start breaking my Overgiver pattern is…

This can be one tiny action. Then, go and do as many of those tiny actions as possible, to start shifting this through little actions that add up to big results.

Want to go even bigger? Book a luxury weekend experience just for you—yes, for *you*—and treat yourself like a queen (or make it happen during school hours, if you can't get childcare!). You need to receive from yourself in order to be able to receive more from others. Put an offer out there, form the intention to make sales and receive money, and then treat yourself to a spa treatment, sleep, and soak—or whatever real luxury feels like for you. Watch the sales roll in whilst you relax.

5

THE IMPOSTER SUCCESS SABOTEUR ARCHETYPE

Let's talk about how the Imposter Success Saboteur is blocking you from receiving your next six figures in your business.

The Imposter Success Saboteur is actually the second most common among the thousands of entrepreneurial women who have taken my free online Success Saboteurs Archetypes assessment. Using my experience in uncovering and healing this Success Saboteur in thousands of women, I am going to help you to understand where the Imposter comes from on a cognitive level by unveiling the patterns and hidden ways in which it shows up so you can start to release it.

The Imposter Success Saboteur was actually my biggest blind spot back in 2020 (after that, the Overprotector definitely took centre stage)! For me, the Imposter Success Saboteur comes up in every uplevel because it is most connected to identity shifts—and our identity needs to shift if we are to become the woman who can receive and hold more, especially when shifting into the identity of a six- or seven-figure business owner (this identity shift needs to happen before you receive it!).

Overview of the Imposter Saboteur

The patterns and blind spots that lie beneath this Imposter Success Saboteur are currently blocking you from receiving your next six figures, regardless of what level you're currently at. It doesn't matter if your next level is the six-figure year, launch, or month; the Imposter Success Saboteur still applies.

It is killing your creativity and your ability to take the most successful, money generating action in your business. Your million-dollar business idea is often hiding behind the Imposter Success Saboteur.

All the Success Saboteurs are interlinked, so there will be some degree of overlap with the Imposter and the other Success Saboteurs we have discussed so far. However, each Saboteur also has its own distinctive wounding and distinctive qualities, and the Imposter is no different. By healing the Imposter Success Saboteur, you are going to be able to start doing business *your* way—the most powerful way!

There are two key ways in which the Imposter shows up. You might resonate with one or both. Either way, we all have this archetype in us.

1. You stop yourself from starting *anything*. You learn without earning, you have content but no purpose/sales, and you have no

clear offers.

2. Things suddenly stop working like they used to. Your sales go down; your marketing stops converting; your launches are just… eek; your revenue goes down; you have no idea who you are anymore. You feel like you are in 'no man's land.'

The Imposter Success Saboteur makes you believe that success comes from outside of you, and is usually down to a lucky break, a fluke, or just chance. You do not recognise your own successes or talents, and you don't truly believe in your abilities. You fear being 'found out' as 'not enough' or not as capable as others think you are.

You find it difficult to trust your own decisions and intuition, and can get stuck in a cycle of signing up for more certificates and courses because you doubt your capabilities and never feel like you know enough. Even when your intuition is giving you great ideas, you ignore it and are always looking to others for guidance (even those who might not know much about your business).

You don't feel truly confident. You pretend you are, but inside, you feel like you are putting on an act or pretence, and are filled with self-doubt. You likely have some issues around trust, whether that is trusting in yourself or others.

If you don't heal this Success Saboteur, you will continue to doubt yourself, your purpose, your ability to deliver results, and your ability to trust a team to support you in your epic mission to change your clients' lives. This is the main Success Saboteur that affects innovation and business expansion, and innovation is key to you becoming a unique leader in your field.

Common Imposter Beliefs and Feelings

Just like with the other Success Saboteurs so far, there are common ways in which the Imposter Success Saboteur shows up to block your six-figure year, launch, or month—and some are universal to every stage. Highlight or note down any of the below common beliefs and feelings associated with the Imposter Success Saboteur that you resonate with.

- 'If people find out who I really am, they won't like me.'
- 'I am not as intelligent or successful as people think I am.'
- 'I can't trust myself to make the right decisions.'
- 'I have to do it so it's 100% perfect, or I have failed.'
- 'I don't really know what I am doing.'
- 'I don't really deserve success because I haven't earned it.' You don't allow things to be easy, and you feel unworthy for not working hard enough.
- 'Why would people want to pay me or work with me?'
- 'I am not good enough.'
- 'It was just luck/the right place or person/a fluke, and I cannot repeat those results again.'
- Feeling full of self-doubt about your abilities and capabilities.
- Fearing that someone will find out you are a fraud or not really who they think you are.
- Fear of failing, fear of making mistakes and losing what you have in your life.
- Believing you do not deserve success as you are not talented or capable enough.

- Feeling you need just one more qualification and then you will be successful
- Feeling not capable or confident enough.

How the Imposter Shows Up at All Levels

There are common ways in which the Imposter shows up generally, whatever stage of your journey you are at right now. Again, just highlight or note down the ones that resonate for you.

- You feel like you are having a massive identity crisis (*Who am I?! What am I here for?! What is my purpose?!*).
- You ignore, deny, or minimise your spiritual side and intuition in your business.
- You feel like you have lost all creativity and struggle to write content.
- Indecisiveness. You have a deep fear of making the wrong decision and the perceived potential consequences.
- You are afraid of letting go of the identity you worked for all your life for (e.g., teacher; social worker) before entrepreneurship, and this is stopping you from going all in.
- You live inauthentically. You are pretending to be someone you are not because you don't believe who you really are is enough. This creates a lack of trust with your audience, because it can create a disconnect.
- You deeply fear making a mistake/getting it wrong and

ultimately facing what others will think if they see you fail.

- You let your partner/parent/friends make all the decisions.
- You ignore your intuition and work with people you've had a bad feeling about—and it turns out to be a bad experience.
- You set excessively high goals for yourself, and when you fail to reach them, you experience self-doubt and anxiety about not measuring up.
- Perfectionism or overworking tendencies.
- Lots of courses that have not been completed.
- Sales droughts and lack of trust in money.
- Trying to be superwoman and do everything yourself.
- Struggles with manifesting as you don't trust the Universe.

How the Imposter Blocks Your Six-Figure Year

At the zero- to six-figure year level, the Imposter generally shows up as struggles to trust yourself and to believe that what you know is enough for you to really make money and impact people.

Highlight or note down any of the below common ways the Imposter shows up to block you from your six-figure year:

- You don't even ask for the sale because you feel like a fraud, or worry that you cannot give the result the prospective client needs.
- You don't share your clients' testimonials because you feel uncomfortable with shouting about how good you are (and hence miss out on the biggest sales attraction tool).

- You spend thousands (if not tens of thousands) on more training because you feel like you don't know enough, or just need one more letter after your name before you can charge properly for what you do.
- You are in a perpetual 'learning without earning' cycle.
- You feel like you must have a coach or someone else's method by your side in order to be successful.
- You struggle to charge enough, even though you are brilliant at what you do, because deep down, you don't believe this is the case, even though clients are always saying so.
- You block yourself from earning money entirely while transitioning from a corporate career to running your own business, or even transitioning from an offline business to an online business.
- You are not being the embodiment of what you sell. This isn't intentional, but can happen when people try to sell what they think will make money.
- A business coach taught you to charge a high price, but you don't have the experience or social proof to justify it yet, so you block sales. You believe you are not qualified enough to charge those prices.
- You are focusing all your attention and effort on activities that don't directly make you money, like podcasts, reels, or Canva images. You spend little or no time on the money-making activities, like creating offers, selling, and marketing.
- You sell a 'method' instead of selling *you* using the method. If you sell a method, you are in competition with others using that

method. The method is only as powerful as the person using it. If you incorporate your unique take on the method, you stand out.

- You create offers that you think will make money rather than creating offers your heart and soul is guiding you to.
- You create before you sell and keep getting stuck in the creation part. (It is better to sell it first and then get paid to create it.)
- You give up if you don't succeed the first time.
- You leave jobs or switch your business direction or product ideas every time you start getting successful with something.
- You change your niche and messaging a lot, leaving your audience confused about what it is you do (heck, even you are confused about what you do!).

A lack of alignment at this level is never intentional, but is very common. Your most successful offers will always be the ones you are already the embodiment of and have results in for yourself.

Your products are more successful and magnetic when they come from your own personal journey and are aligned with your soul purpose. You are the social proof! When you do something because you love it and are passionate about it, that is money-making energy. Every piece of marketing you release should lead to one of your services, but money-making activities feel uncomfortable for the Imposter because there is a deep fear of success and of failure underpinning these actions.

How the Imposter Blocks Your Six-Figure Launch

At the six-figure launch level, some of those struggles around you being able to trust yourself are shifting. Now, the biggest way in which the Imposter shows up is through struggles to trust others to support you with your growth, struggles to trust in the Universe to support you and struggles to trust in processes and change.

Highlight or note down any of the below common behaviours associated with the Imposter Success Saboteur that resonate for you:

- You struggle to hire and delegate, as you do not trust others to do the job well, and so try to do it all yourself.
- Your signature program isn't feeling aligned anymore, but you are scared to change it, so you keep selling it, even though you feel disconnected from it. (People can sense this!)
- Your million-dollar idea already came to you in a dream/while you were washing your hair/while you were having a walk one day, and you ignored it, because you do not trust the things coming through you.
- You look at others who are having six-figure launches and believe they have something magical you don't.
- You feel triggered by others owning their talents, gifts, and prices.
- You don't trust yourself to generate sales and income on the investments you make.
- You don't trust the launch process you have decided upon and switch strategies instead of following one strategy through to completion.

- You start buying a ton of courses and coaching about how to have a great launch, and you get even more confused as you listen to input from too many different people instead of doing it your way.
- Whenever a launch starts to become more successful, you create something new, reinvent the wheel or quickly pull the plug on it, because deep down you fear success.

It's very normal for my clients to heal their Success Saboteurs in the Ultimate Uplevel Academy (especially the Imposter) and shift into a different business or variation of the business they came in with, because they create a business more aligned to their soul and true purpose. They start listening to their intuition and it explodes their success. Take my client Jess: she had wanted to move her business in a new direction for a while, but her Imposter had stopped her. She finally took action on the nudges of her soul and launched a multi-six-figure revenue stream.

How the Imposter Blocks Your Six-Figure Month

When you reach consistent six-figure months, that means you officially have a seven-figure business. The seven-figure woman identity you need to step into to receive and hold six-figure months is very different to the six-figure woman identity you need to step into to receive and hold a six-figure year—ten times different, to be exact! It sends your Imposter wild if you haven't done the inner work to become the woman who can receive and hold that next level. At this level, your Imposter shows up as not trusting that level of success and, specifically, not trusting that you can handle or hold it. You don't trust your bigger purpose or, as Gabby Bernstein would say, that the Universe has your back. Getting to this level of financial success happens when you trust and co-create with the Universe and are living your true soul purpose.

This level of success quite frankly scares the hell out of you. You are afraid to act, and you stay stuck where you are. It all feels too big.

When I did my eight-figure rebrand in 2022, I first stepped into the identity of the eight-figure woman. Things shifted fast for me, and soon, I was celebrating my first half-a-million-dollar sales month. I was initially excited over the amount of clarity I was feeling. It felt so amazing to know exactly what I needed to do to evolve myself and my work into the next level. But then I felt fear. It all felt too big! *Who am I to have an eight-figure business?!*

Have you ever felt like your idea is too big or too scary, and so you started to talk yourself out of it and, ultimately, decided to stay where you are—where you are comfortable and safe? This stops you from evolving into that seven- or eight-figure brand.

You evolve first. Then, your business follows.

There are common ways the Imposter shows up at this level. Again, just highlight or note down the ones that resonate for you as you are reading through.

- Lack of trust in success.
- Your true success and earning potential scares the fuck out of you. The thought of the 'bigness' that is possible keeps you stuck where you are.

- You don't trust yourself to make million-dollar hires or fires.
- You are nervous to become the woman who makes that kind of money.
- You hesitate to rebrand into a seven- or eight-figure brand because you are scared to change what feels comfortable and safe.
- You've gotten comfortable, and things that used to work have stopped working. The program you created five years ago isn't selling like it used to. You know you need to update the program, but the fear of the time and effort involved (and the risk that comes with changing what is 'good enough as is') is stopping you.
- You start looking outside of yourself for the answers. You delegate your power and slip out of the energy that got you to where you are.
- You feel that you are not worthy compared to others in your industry, so you try to do things their way, mimicking them and pushing yourself harder, faster, and further to try and measure up. Your Imposter makes you slip into hustler mode.

Where the Imposter Comes From

The Imposter Success Saboteur Archetype develops in response to multiple wounds of the heart. It is a survival strategy your mind and heart create when you experience something as a child that wounds you, specifically by causing you to believe you are not enough, doubt yourself, question your perception of reality or believe or feel that you cannot trust yourself and your abilities. It developed to help keep us safe in some way as a child, but as an adult it holds us back—especially in our businesses!

Many things can trigger the Imposter Success Saboteur. Here are some example situations/circumstances to help you explore where your Imposter Success Saboteur might have come from. Highlight or note down any of the below common situations associated with the Imposter Success Saboteur that you resonate with.

- Growing up in a family where appearances and achievement were important.
- Being gaslit or told you are wrong constantly.
- Receiving a good grade but a parent still asking, 'Why didn't you get better?'
- Having to pretend everything is okay in school when home life is bad, or vice versa.
- Hiding basic things so you don't get in trouble.
- Doing something a parent told you not to, and hurting yourself or failing in some way in the process.
- Pretending you could do something that you couldn't do to avoid embarrassment.
- Receiving harsh punishments for normal childhood behaviours.
- Being punished for something you didn't do because no one believed your innocence.
- Someone constantly telling you that you are not good enough.
- Beating yourself up over wrong decisions and believing that you can't trust yourself to make good decisions.
- Anything that causes you to doubt your reality, including narcissistic relationships, abusive relationships in adulthood, or abusive childhoods.

- Seeing your parent crying and knowing something was wrong, but they pretended they were okay, overriding your judgement.
- Being compared to a sibling you felt (or you were told) was better than you.
- Believing you must have committed fraud or deceived someone in some way, or you wouldn't have the success you do.
- Being told or believing you are not capable.
- Living on eggshells; never knowing what is right or wrong and developing a fear of making mistakes because of the unpredictable responses of a parent or a partner.
- Pretending to be someone else to fit in or feel like you belong.

Reflect on and recognise how these patterns are showing up in your relationship with money and in your life and business today. In particular, this Success Saboteur can massively influence your relationship with money, because you don't trust money or the fact that it will stay or show up consistently.

Where the Imposter Came from For Me

When I was younger, I was gaslighted many times about the abuse I was experiencing. I was made to think it was all in my head, punished for 'lying', and repeatedly not believed about my experiences. This made me doubt myself. Now, after many years of therapy and decades of post-traumatic stress disorder (PTSD) nightmares (which I thankfully no longer have), I know without a shadow of a doubt that everything I experienced was very real, but as children, we believe the adults in our world unconditionally, so we think, *I must be wrong, not the adult.* We start to question ourselves. I had also been very psychic and open to spiritual experiences as a child. A lot of the spiritual side of things scared me and I closed it down.

I was always a high achiever. As a way to cope, I threw myself into my education. As mentioned previously, I am a double-award-winning psychology graduate and an innovator, and I created lifesaving initiatives in homelessness services that became published in professional magazines. I identified as a 'high achiever' and hustled in order to feel good about myself, yet I never actually *did* have true confidence in my skills or potential. Any time I got a new job or achieved something big, I would put it down to luck, chance, a fluke, or me being in the right place at the right time.

My Six-Figure Year

My first ever business was a product business, and it quite literally started in 2014 with a dream about making natural peanut butter and selling it to others. I woke up that very morning, saw a white feather in my car, took it as a sign and started my food brand. Guilt Free Goodies launched with nothing but a Vitamix bought from a small inheritance after my great-nan passed away and a passion for creating healthy treats that tasted good. I was also opening up to my spiritual gifts again at this point in my life. Years later, when I wanted to expand my business into coaching too, even though I had many years of professional experience in transformation, certifications, trainings, and degrees (including master's degrees), I still felt that I wasn't qualified enough to coach. I felt like I needed another certification in order to be deemed capable or enough to sell coaching online.

I felt like I was starting again. My Imposter made me ignore all my transferable skills. Basically, when I transitioned from the offline world to the online world, it took me time to recognise that I was highly qualified already! My Imposter contributed to me undercharging and I even went through a phase of copying or being too heavily influenced by others around me who I looked up to because I was struggling to find my own identity, not realising that it could have got me into all sorts of legal trouble. *Who was Natasha?* I had a health business initially and I kept hearing this intuitive voice telling me to work with business owners—but not as a business coach. I felt a strong intuitive pull to training in a hypnotherapy-based modality, initially to help other women with food addictions. It was when I followed those universal nudges that my true purpose started to unfold. Women started to come to me for subconscious work around unlocking success in their businesses, and my business exploded to my first six-figure year in 2018.

My Six-Figure Launch

As my business continued to grow, I made a few decisions I later started to beat myself up about. Ones where people ran off with thousands of pounds without delivering, or with wounded mentors that I had bad experiences with. I blamed myself for these things, berating myself for my decision to invest in the wrong people. There was one especially where my healer had warned me not to invest in a particular person because of their dark energy. I, thinking I knew best, decided to invest anyway. And it went badly. Now, I have managed to take the gold from those experiences and truly believe every investment gives us the lesson we need, not necessarily the one we want. But my self-trust started to be eroded by these experiences that I blamed myself for.

As a result of this, I started looking outside of myself for the answers instead of turning inwards. I invested more money in things and people I didn't really need. I lost all clarity in my business, and felt like I had no idea who I was or who I was meant to serve. For a while, I stopped trusting myself entirely. Even now, when my Imposter Success Saboteur comes up strong, I notice that same pattern of frantically looking outside of myself for multiple people to invest in who can help me. I eventually recognise my Imposter coming up and realise I have everything I need inside. In fact, I use my own therapy recordings to heal myself and connect to my guides, the Universe and my higher self for all of the best business advice I have ever received!

I channelled a new subconscious healing method (HeartHealing) at the end of 2019 that was getting never-witnessed-before rapid results with my clients. The Success Saboteur Archetypes then came to me in a dream (notice a pattern here?) in January 2020, and for a long time, I sat on this idea and didn't do anything with it. I knew it was going to be big, and that was a scary thought! Normally, I act fast on my intuition, but it took me another six months to bring this work to the world in July 2020—which is when my Success Imprinting method and the Ultimate Uplevel Academy were also born, and my business exploded to new levels. When I healed my Imposter Success Saboteur and turned inwards again, my business grew exponentially and I had my first two six-figure launches at the same time!

My Six-Figure Months

After quite literally following my dreams to launch the Success Saboteur Archetypes work into the world, I started having consistent six-figure months, thanks to healing my Imposter Success Saboteur. I was fully owning *my* gifts, *my* methods, and *my* way of doing things, and, sure enough, that became my first million-dollar year in business.

I believe everything happens for a reason, and those things were meant to happen to help me bring the power of healing the Imposter Success Saboteur and betrayal wounds to my clients.

Your intuition is the best coach you will ever have. It is completely free, but you do need to be able to trust her. Since I started really embracing my spirituality more in my business, I have developed lots of ways of connecting spiritually and taking action on my spiritual side. My most successful ideas and courses have impacted thousands of people. My business has completely skyrocketed, and the same happens for my clients, too. In my Ultimate Uplevel Academy, this work is called the Intuition and Innovation Experience. It is one of the most transformational parts of the Ultimate Uplevel Academy.

Your intuition is trying to guide you to your soul's purpose in life. When you are in alignment with this, six-figure leaps will become easy, because the money is the reward for your service. The more you are in alignment with your legacy, the richer you will become, but you have to take action on it, even when you cannot see the full path ahead.

When I had my second baby, I had an identity crisis that comes with being a mum of two. I (naively) thought I would be immune to this as a second-time mum, but, sure enough, those old, familiar feelings from my first pregnancy returned. 'Who am I, as a mother of two, to own a seven-figure business? Who am I now?'

I had recently rebranded to the eight-figure level, and rebrands are key times for the Imposter to come up, because you are shifting into a new identity. You are not just rebranding your business; you are rebranding yourself, and that can feel scary. Every time you rebrand, you are stepping into a higher version of yourself.

At the resurfacing of my Imposter, my growth plateaued a bit. I lost my creativity, and found I couldn't write content in the same way. But I had been through this before, just before my first million-dollar year. I knew I had to ride it out, because something big was on the other side. After some growing pains, everything feels like it is expanding and evolving again.

Sure enough, the power of my work expanded.

I debuted my first ever live 'Your Next Six Figures' experience with a full knowing I would turn it into this book one day. Over nine hundred people signed up organically within forty-eight hours—more than I have ever had sign up to anything before. Then, during that group coaching experience, I had my first six-figure *day*. I secured my first $65,000 sale—with ease! The client was an incredible woman who could not wait to pay me; she was *grateful* to spend that money on me.

I could never have dreamed of being the woman who could charge that—and I put that offer out with absolute confidence it was worth double that amount. She made $74k back in one month of our one-year journey together.

Healing all the dimensions of the wounds at the root of the Imposter Success Saboteur was key for me being able to trust and follow my intuitive ideas, and to trust and follow my spirituality that brought me my greatest successes. It was key to me being able to trust and develop a team to support me and my clients as we grew. It was key to me being able to trust that I can just take the first step without yet being able to see the full journey.

The Imposter Success Saboteur wants to see the entire plan before moving forward, but when it *does* see the full journey ahead, it can get so overwhelmed that you don't move forward at all. So much more can happen for you when you don't expect to know the whole journey and you just trust the process and take one step at a time, keep moving forward, and act on those intuitive ideas that keep coming to you. I've never had a business plan; I have just taken one action, one step, every day, and healed all the things I identified as sabotaging me and holding me back.

How much further would you move forward if you just took one step forward every day, instead of staying stuck in inaction?

How the Imposter Looks When It Is Healed

When you heal your Imposter Success Saboteur, you are finally able to trust in yourself and your gifts, innovate your legacy work and show up as the unique leader you are. It creates dramatic change in every area of your life. Specifically:

- Your intuition skyrockets and you start to follow your soul, which leads to more success.
- You stop spending tons of money on coaches and courses, because you know that everything you need is inside of you.
- You innovate and create with ease. Courses and methods are suddenly easy to write, and you stand out as a pioneer in your field.
- You take action even when you don't know what the full path ahead looks like.
- You have rock solid confidence in the fact that you are incredible at what you do, and your audience senses this and can't wait to buy from you as a result.
- You trust and listen to yourself more than anyone else.
- You know your business better than anyone else does.
- You trust your gut about decisions and investments, and you trust there is no such thing as mistakes; only lessons.
- You start to show the world more of who you are. You show up authentically and no longer feel like you have to pretend to be someone else. This is magnetic energy.
- You are able to build a strong, successful team to support your six-figure leaps, on repeat.

The healing of the Imposter Success Saboteur is, without a doubt, my favourite part of the Ultimate Uplevel Academy, as it is often the work the women didn't know they needed and has a bigger impact than they expected. They download new courses, new methods, and new innovations that are revolutionary in their fields. They unlock their million-dollar business ideas and come out with a business that reflects who they really are, making more money than ever before. Self-trust changes everything. It is beautiful to witness.

Oftentimes, women feel like Imposters because they are trying to be like men; to create success the 'masculine' way. This doesn't work, because your soul and intuition hold the key to your success; to the feminine gifts that you have disconnected from and that your true power lies behind.

You cannot fully trust yourself if you are denying your spiritual self. Accept all of you, and your success will soar.

Gifts Behind the Imposter

The biggest gift that lies behind the Imposter is the Gift of Genius. The stronger the Imposter, the more of a genius you really are underneath it! You have untapped genius that will revolutionise the world. You are here to change the world through your unique genius and innovations. People will write books and make films about your contributions to the world, and you will go down in the history books. The problem is that without healing the Imposter, this 'bigness' of your calling will scare you into staying exactly where you are right now.

To get you started with healing your Imposter, please first know that no matter what, you cannot fail. Everything is a lesson. You are divinely supported in everything you do; you just need to connect to that divine support, trust it and take action on it.

Other gifts that lie behind a healed Imposter are;

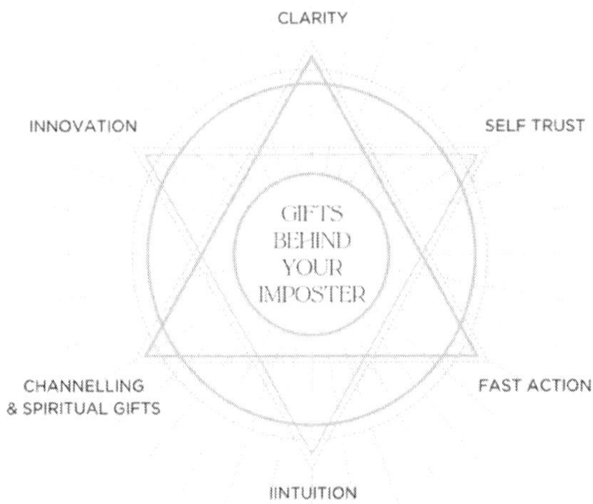

Figure 6: The Imposter Success Saboteur

Healing the Imposter

Over the course of this chapter, you have learned how the Imposter Success Saboteur is showing up for you. On a scale of one to ten (with ten being the most), rate how much the Imposter is blocking you from receiving your next six figures.

The unveiling process in this chapter will already have created significant shifts for you around this Success Saboteur on multiple levels of healing. Let's take this deeper now with some more healing tasks.

Mind Healing

Let's start to prove the fact that those pesky Imposter beliefs you uncovered are, in fact, BS!

List every certificate/qualification/achievement you have ever accomplished in your life. Think back as far as you can remember. This includes:

- School/out-of-school activities.
- Work/work training.
- Awards won.
- Business trainings/degrees/college courses.

Add up the total value of this list in terms of the cost and time. (You can estimate old stuff, or even use Google for a rough price.) Tally up the time and money you have invested in becoming the current version of yourself. How much have you really invested in yourself and in your life? Think about everything: further education; work; training; awards… and let's not forget the time you've spent honing your craft and all the business courses and coaches you have invested in, too! I can imagine there are hundreds of hours, and thousands (if not tens or hundreds of thousands) that you have invested in becoming you with all of the knowledge, wisdom and experience you hold.

That is what you are bringing to your clients and business. Every single qualification, achievement, and investment you have added to your life has contributed to what you bring to the people you are here to serve. That's not luck, and that's not you 'winging it'. You are *not* a fraud! You bring *so much* to your business.

You already are an expert; you're just not recognising or owning it—yet.

Heart Healing

Look back at the situations you resonated with around the Imposter Success Saboteur. Is there a common person who keeps coming up repeatedly? This indicates a key relationship that you would benefit from healing, to help release the Overgiver Success Saboteur. You can begin this process by writing a therapeutic letter to that person releasing any anger or hurt you feel towards them and taking your power and self-trust back. Read it out loud as if saying it to them for extra emotional release.

Soul Healing

Write a healing letter to the part of you that first started to doubt herself and her abilities. Tell her what she needs to hear from you in order to let go of this pattern and trust in herself, her skills, and her gifts, and to own her genius.

Read this letter out loud to yourself, as if you were reading it aloud to her. Afterwards, visualise yourself hugging her and merging with her as you become one.

Energy Healing

Who do you need to evolve into to become the woman who receives her next six figures with ease? Is it the six-figure woman? The seven-figure woman? Or even the eight-figure woman? If you were already her, how would you be showing up? What would you be doing differently? What advice would she give you?

Action Healing

Look at those things you would be doing differently in the previous task. Which of these things can you take action on now? Brainstorm some more tiny actions. Then, go and do as many of those tiny actions as possible to embody being the woman who receives her next six figures now.

Want to go bigger? Write out a list of all the ideas you have had that were so big they scared you. Maybe there's one big thing that you've always wanted to do—one thing your inner coach is guiding you towards—but your logical mind keeps finding excuses to not make it happen. That is your million-dollar idea. This is the one you should be focusing on. Decide to take the first step towards making it happen. Maybe it's applying for a particular trademark, or discussing the idea with someone you trust. All the Universe needs is for you to claim it—and then the next step will appear.

6

THE OUTCAST SUCCESS SABOTEUR ARCHETYPE

Firstly, I just want to witness you and congratulate you for making it this far. This is deep work, and it can be uncomfortable seeing all the ways we have been unknowingly sabotaging ourselves and where they may have come from. Know that even just reading this book, you are already making huge shifts to change this. We have two more Success Saboteur Archetypes left. Keep going.

In this chapter, we are diving deep into the Outcast Success Saboteur Archetype. I will unveil what it is, show you how it is blocking you from receiving your next six figures, and, most importantly, how to heal it so you can unlock all the gifts, wealth and success currently hiding behind it. The Outcast Success Saboteur is blocking your next six figures by impacting your ability to sell more, be seen more and scale more.

The Outcast Success Saboteur is about so much more than being afraid to be visible. It blocks your money, sales, and marketing, and keeps any group experiences you launch plateaued in terms of your income and how many clients you can hold at any one time. As I said before, you can't just *achieve* your next six figures; you also need to be able to *receive* it. It also keeps you hiding those spiritual gifts you unveiled beneath your Imposter too (the Witch Wound is totally linked to this saboteur!).

Overview of The Outcast Saboteur

Awareness is the first stage of change, so I am going to help you understand this Success Saboteur so you can start to release it. If you have a strong Outcast Success Saboteur, you are deeply driven to avoid feeling the pain of rejection.

There are two key ways in which the Outcast Success Saboteur shows up:

1. Fear of being seen (resulting in avoidance of all visibility) and fears/limits around selling.
2. Being visible, but not visible as who you 'really are' (as it's easier to be rejected for who you are not than for who you really are).

This is the key Success Saboteur in affecting sales. Even if you are making a lot of sales right now, you could be making *more* sales. Or you may go through periods of withdrawing from selling and so it isn't consistent.

If your Outcast Success Saboteur Archetype is strong, you may feel like you have never really fitted in, and deep down, you crave to feel accepted and like you belong somewhere. Your deep fear of rejection causes you to hide your true self from the world. This means that anything that involves being seen or speaking out is especially difficult for you, as it affects your sense of safety. You either try to avoid it completely or you pretend to be someone else when you have to be visible in order to prevent your true self from feeling rejected. You keep yourself small, because you believe that nobody is interested in what you have to say, and that 'hiding' or being invisible will keep you safe.

Despite this, you have dreams of being more visible, speaking on stages, writing books, serving thousands, and creating a huge ripple of change in the world. These things all come with a lot of visibility, and a *lot* of impact.

If you don't heal this Success Saboteur, these things will continue to feel like a struggle, and your fears will stop you from being visible and seen in a way that converts to your next six-figure leap. It will also block your ability to connect more deeply to your audience and convert followers into buyers, because when you aren't showing up as your authentic self, you are unable to connect with others through your content, whether written or verbal. This can impact romantic relationships and friendships too: you often reject people before they have a chance to reject you.

Common Outcast Beliefs and Feelings

I am going to share the most common beliefs and feelings that indicate you have an Outcast Success Saboteur holding you back from your next six figures. As you are reading them, ask yourself, 'Does this feel right or wrong for me?' and highlight or make a note of any of the ones that resonate for you. After noting the ones that resonate with you, you may want to reflect on any other ways this Success Saboteur shows up in your beliefs and feelings and make a note of those too.

- 'If I am visible, people will gossip or laugh at me. I may say something wrong or embarrass myself.'
- 'Being invisible keeps me safe.'
- 'My opinions don't matter. They are not important.'
- 'It's not safe to stand out. It's not safe to be noticed. It's not safe to express myself. It's not safe to be seen as having it all.'
- 'I don't have anything to say that people want to hear.'
- 'I don't fit in. I don't belong. I am alone.'
- Being seen for who you really are is not safe because there is a risk of being judged or rejected.
- Feeling like there must be something wrong with you.
- Struggling to see why others may be interested in you and what you have to say.
- Feeling safer in small groups.
- You fear being seen as different or unique (because fitting in feels safer).
- You may feel not safe to be seen as spiritual, so hide this side of

you.

How the Outcast Shows Up at All Levels

There are common ways the Outcast shows up generally, whatever stage of your six-figure journey you are in right now. Again, just highlight or note down the ones that resonate for you as you are reading through.

- Hypersensitivity to client complaints and any perceived criticism. Perceived criticism can also be a trigger in family relationships.
- Feeling down for days if you get a 'no' about something. This interrupts or stops your flow, and even your launch.
- Not being able to lose weight, or suddenly gaining weight as a way of hiding in your own body.
- Only feeling comfortable in small social groups.
- Isolating yourself in relationships and friendships, almost as if to prove to yourself that you are an outcast.
- Worrying you'll eventually have haters and trolls like the celebrities or high achieving coaches you follow.
- Subconsciously being afraid that your own family will reject you if you become 'too' anything: too successful; too rich; too big for your boots. You worry that you won't belong if you don't fit in with their struggle story.
- Relying on people to find you instead of putting yourself out

there.[5]

- Rejecting others before they can reject you, especially in personal relationships and friendships.
- Taking it personally when someone doesn't sign up after saying they would.
- Not owning how good you are at what you do.
- The Chameleon Effect: whoever you are talking to, you begin to mirror them slightly, speaking and acting like them, becoming like them to help them like you instead of just being yourself.

Now, let's look at how the Outcast blocks you from that six-figure year, launch, or month. Pay attention to all the different levels discussed, as the symptoms can be fluid across them, and even though you are not there yet, you may notice something that resonates with you (or identify something to look out for!).

How the Outcast Blocks Your Six-Figure Year

At this level, the Outcast mostly shows up as blocks to visibility and sales. Highlight or note down any of the following that resonate with you:

- Feeling timid, fearful or blocked around selling.
- Struggling with sales calls. They go on forever and still end in a no!

---

[5]Expecting people to find you is not a reliable business strategy! It is something that happens naturally sometimes, but these flukes don't give you any control over your income.

- Not asking for the sale enough (e.g., putting one post out and then feeling like you've failed, so stop talking about it as you think nobody is interested).
- Not being visible enough and thinking one post a week is enough to market your business (it isn't).
- Deep visibility fears that show up as 'hiding' in business (not sharing stories, not marketing, not sharing client results, not doing videos).
- Deleting your posts if nobody likes or comments or just after you have posted it.
- Vague or 'vanilla' marketing. You water down your true opinions and voice to be more accepted by everyone.
- Buying a group program and disappearing/ghosting the provider or hiding from taking part.
- Hiding your prices 'til you get on calls, as you worry what people will think (especially your family).
- Difficulty humble bragging about your results (or even sharing them).
- Inconsistent marketing. One week you show up every day, then you disappear for weeks or months on end.
- Difficulties networking and connecting with others.

The truth is there is a part of you that is *so terrified* of hearing a 'no' (a.k.a., getting rejected) that you often don't even ask for the sale (or don't ask enough). This is blocking your financial success, because *you cannot receive sales without asking for them*. You might get one sale here or there from a referral or the Universe, but that is not a method that will allow you to be in control of your business. Financial freedom doesn't come from the amount of money you have in the bank; it comes with the knowledge that you have the power to make money any time you want to—and that comes from selling, and having the confidence to sell every day; the confidence to put your offers out and not stop selling until there are no spots left in your program; to not take it personally if something doesn't sell, because it's not about you (even though you might believe it is!); to take down and tweak the offer and try again. Your Outcast is holding you back from showing up to sell, and the less you sell, the less you serve! The less you serve, the less you receive.

Anytime someone tells me that their sales have gone down, I peek at their social media, and I *always* find that they are not asking for the sale enough. Sometimes, this cycle can have you discouraged for days or weeks. You might even consider giving up your business altogether because you are so deeply affected by it, when really, you are not allowing yourself to be seen enough. It is as simple as healing your Outcast and asking for the sale every day.

You find it difficult to brag about your results, or even share them at all, even though you know you need to share the amazing results you get with your clients; people need to see social proof in order to trust you to buy from you.

If you are feeling discouraged by this long list, rest assured that I have done all these things during my own business journey (and I now own businesses that collectively make millions!). There is no shame in any of this; it is actually normal, and is a part of every entrepreneur's journey to success.

How the Outcast Blocks Your Six-Figure Launch

Each Success Saboteur will resurface as you reach each new level, because there will be new aspects to heal that you weren't able to see until you reach that level. The Outcast is no different.

At this level, you have overcome some of those initial fears and difficulties around being seen and selling. Now, your Outcast shows up in two specific ways: fear of size and fear of intimacy.

Here are some more specific ways in which the Outcast shows at this level. Highlight or note down any that resonate for you:

- You don't feel safe enough to join masterminds or large groups because you find them 'too big' or 'too intimate'. (If you don't feel comfortable being in a large group as a member, you will never feel safe to run a large group.)
- You subconsciously keep your group programs small because you fear larger groups/feel safer in smaller groups. This limits your capacity to hold more people.
- You struggle to do the videos that you need to do in order to move from a one-to-one coaching model to one-to-many model.
- You try to give everyone in your programs a one-to-one-level service. This is draining on your time and energy.
- You have fears around building and growing a team because you are the self-proclaimed 'lone wolf', and you worry that you won't fit in with your own team. So, you try to either isolate yourself from them or not build a team at all.
- You have visibility hangovers. You show up, things go well, you

are everywhere on social media... and then you disappear like a puff of smoke.

- You disappear for weeks after a launch because you feel like the life was sucked from you during it.

Your group numbers will always stay plateaued to what feels safe to you. Much like the Overprotector impacts your capacity to hold more success, the Outcast limits your capacity to hold more clients. Energetically, you are not showing the Universe that you are capable of holding the things that come with a six-figure launch—i.e., more people, more relationships, and bigger groups!

My client Gaby Abrams came to me while she was having consistent $30-50k months. She wanted to work with me specifically on expanding the capacity to hold more people in her group programs and on unlocking six figure months. Once we worked together one-to-one to heal her Outcast Success Saboteur and the heart wound underneath it, she was able to *triple* the amount of people coming into her group programs. The fear was gone. She very quickly expanded to six-figure months from this within just a couple of months of working together. You can watch her inspiring interview on my YouTube channel, along with many of the other clients I have mentioned in this book.

How the Outcast Blocks Your Six-Figure Month

At the six-figure month level, the Outcast shows up as the fear of becoming globally known and seen, and a fear of being publicly outcast by other women. Even though you *want* to be globally known and to make millions, subconsciously, you feel that you will be in danger if you are seen as ultra-successful. The danger isn't necessarily physical, but the fear of the emotional pain and wounds of the heart that risk being triggered by women being jealous and being publicly attacked or humiliated; with verbal attacks by haters and online trolls. There is a deep fear of being seen as successful and then being punished and attacked or harmed *publicly* as a result. This has links with the Overprotector Success Saboteur, who comes up to protect you when you fear others' reactions to your success. But the key difference with the Outcast is that you fear being *seen* as successful and the attack being something *public*.

Here are the ways the Outcast shows up at this level. Highlight or note down any that resonate with you:

- Isolating yourself from networking and no longer growing your audience, slipping back into the role of the 'lone wolf'.
- Investing in big programs to build networks and start expanding, only to not show up or maximise on the investment.
- Being scared of charging your new, current prices to your old clients, significantly undercharging your long-standing clients, and not moving them onto newer prices.
- Avoiding leading your team (i.e., 'hiding' from them) and trying to delegate the leadership to others.
- Feeling hurt and rejected when clients don't re-sign.
- Fearing being attacked by other women publicly if your success triggers them, so you hide your success and feel anxious about anyone knowing your earnings.

- Feeling conflicted around raising your prices to premium prices.
- Publicly speaking about your faults and failings so others don't think you are 'too perfect'.
- Fear of your work being stolen so hiding all of your unique ideas and talents behind the paywall.
- Fear working with other women on your level in case they say something bad about you.

Where the Outcast Comes From

Looking at root causes can understandably be emotional for some. We are going to look at situations that can lead to the development of the Outcast Success Saboteur, and different ones will hold different emotional charges for you. Remember that my team and I are here to support you (you can find how to connect with us on the Resources page at the back of this book), and that the reason why we are bringing these to the surface is because knowing where our sabotaging patterns come from can be a great source of release and healing that can create the freedom we desire.

I am highly experienced in working with all forms of trauma. Many doctors, psychologists, psychotherapists and other healing professionals often come to me as they know I can hold them. If you have gone through deeper traumas, you have a safe space to talk about them in my world.

The Outcast Success Saboteur Archetype is activated as a survival strategy when a child a) does not feel safe to be seen and/or b) does not 'fit in', whether at home or in school. This could have been because you were bullied or moved schools a lot, or because you felt like you didn't truly belong in your family because you felt so different to them. Perhaps you were intentionally excluded because you had a toxic family and were treated as the 'scapegoat', or you experienced or witnessed aggression or abuse in the family home. All these circumstances lead to a belief 'there must be something wrong with me' or 'I am not safe'. You struggle to accept yourself for who you are and hide to keep yourself safe.

Here are some more situations that may have led to the development of the Outcast in your childhood. Read them with an open mind and note down any that resonate for you:

- You were told that you were 'too much' or 'too loud'.
- You were told off for being 'too big for your boots' or 'too confident'.
- You were not allowed to speak unless you were spoken to; you grew up in an environment where 'children should be seen and not heard'.
- You felt like the 'odd one out', or were directly told you were, either at school or at home. You might have been even intentionally left out (e.g., as a stepchild).
- You always felt different from others and never fit in.[6]
- You were scapegoated as a child.
- You had angry or abusive parents or siblings, so tried to stay out of their way.
- You witnessed violence in the home.
- You were punished for playing, being noisy, or just being a child (even unintentional wounds can leave scars).

---

[6]Every child feels that they don't fit in; they just didn't know that all children felt that way.

- You were bullied or suffered abuse.
- You had an unsafe home or school environment.
- You were publicly humiliated or laughed at.
- You were mocked and made to dim your light.
- Someone was jealous of your confidence.
- You experienced racism or discrimination.
- You got an answer wrong in front of your peers in school and felt embarrassed.
- You found it safer to hide or not be noticed.
- You were not allowed to have opinions, or your opinions were not considered important; your opinions were not acknowledged, or were ignored all together.
- You were an introvert.
- You had (or suspect you had) undiagnosed neurodiversity that made you feel different.

You may have had experiences like this in childhood, to find they've then shown up in your business relationships with bosses, clients, mentors, and peers, and in your romantic relationships. This is normal, because these patterns repeat until we have healed the root causes (the heart wounds) and the Success Saboteurs that have come from them. Only then do we get to break and stop these patterns.

Where the Outcast Came from For Me

I want to share my own journey with a *huge* Outcast Success Saboteur so that you can see how I overcame it to grow the multi-seven-figure business I have today.

My Six-Figure Year

When I first started my business, I *could not* do videos at all. I had *deep* visibility fears and I would actually have a physical trauma response, and my body would shake and sweat any time I tried to create a video.

I was an overweight teen who was the target for the school bullies. I tried to hide behind my glasses and my weight. 'Out of sight, out of mind', as they say.

I used to describe myself as a 'wallflower'. I was 'the quiet one' in my friend group. I was extremely introverted, and was always made to feel like I had nothing good to say, even by my so-called 'friends'. As a result, I didn't speak much at all.

I hated drawing attention to myself because I had such low self-worth. I believed I had nothing worth saying. I would often hide in the toilets to eat my lunch so that I wouldn't be judged, publicly humiliated and picked on even more for my weight.

To add to all that, I experienced chronic long-term abuse all the way through my childhood, and it was easier and safer for me to be 'invisible' and to hide from them. My survival strategy was to stay out of their sight and out of their way. I was also the 'scapegoat' and 'odd one out' at home as the stepchild in the family.

What beliefs did this give me?

- Being visible is dangerous, risky, harmful, and even deadly.
- Being invisible is safer.
- No one is interested in what I have to say.
- I fear being judged or rejected.
- No one will save me, so I have to protect myself.

My grandfather also instilled in me the belief that 'girls should be seen and not heard', a common saying for his generation. So I took that to heart as a child, too. But I knew I *had* to get comfortable with being seen and heard on video, or I wouldn't be able to scale my business to impact more people. I knew that I had to move away from constant one-to-one work to reach that first six-figure milestone. I did a lot of work around healing from the childhood bullying and gradually did more and more videos and put myself forward for guest expert workshops in other people's communities. It was slow (as I hadn't discovered heart wound work at this point) but I was able to create my first live webinar to sell my old signature program, and had a £35k launch! Although, I chuckle at the fact I hid behind slides and didn't have my face onscreen for several years. To this day I don't do a lot of video marketing, but reserve being on camera for my live experiences and group programs. Much to my surprise, people love me on camera! Let that be your evidence that you don't have to be dancing on socials to make money, or be on live for your audience all the time to receive and hold your next six figures.

My Six-Figure Launch

After my first six-figure month, everything came crashing down around me. Part of this was linked to my experience of being shamed within a community I had felt like I had belonged to. I chose to leave that community (and it really was the best thing for me) but felt unable to show up for a while with the same confidence I'd had before. My Outcast massively came up to protect me (as did my Overprotector and Imposter!). For the first time, I felt resistance to selling, as if I had lost my ability to sell. Of course, this affected my income too. Six figures in one go (like in a launch or month) felt unsafe. So it was some time again before I felt ready to receive that level.

You, too, may have already had a six-figure launch or a six-figure year and then found that you have gone backwards again after experiencing a traumatic situation.

After the experience of having my first six-figure month and then regressing, that was when, at the start of 2020, I innovated HeartHealing and uncovered the first four Success Saboteurs. Six months later, after I went on my own deep journey with the Success Saboteurs and overcame my fears of selling and being seen for my own unique body of work, I received not one, but *two* six-figure launches at the same time.

My Six-Figure Months

Ever since I have consistently worked on healing the layers of my Success Saboteur Archetypes, I have consistently had six-figure and multi-six-figure months, and lots of six-figure launches and even multi-six figure launches.

In 2021, I made over $2 million in cash across my companies with a mailing list of only two thousand five hundred people. This is not normal. Most people with that kind of turnover have an audience of tens or hundreds of thousands.

How did I do it? Being authentically me, thanks to feeling safe to be seen for who I was.

That shy, introverted, bullied, and abused younger me turned into a leading Success Mastery Coach and a Transformational Healer, impacting female entrepreneurs all over the world. I am recognized as a leader in my niche and have won multiple awards, including Top 100, Top 35 Under 35, and Creative Entrepreneur of the Year, and I was highly commended by Women of the Future for my innovative methods, second place to an incredible woman who had innovated cancer detection machines for hospitals.

I went from physically shaking while recording a video to actually hosting an event where I spoke onstage. I have the confidence to travel the world networking and lead bestselling book projects. I am continuously, confidently creating videos and showing up on livestreams for group programs so I can impact more women. I've been featured many times in the media and was interviewed by the Welsh government about my work on healing trauma. I was even invited to an audience with Hilary Clinton when she visited Wales!

If there is one thing I want you to know, you can survive your biggest fear and alchemise that shit into gold. I (and my business) survived my worst fear after feeling *very* publicly attacked by someone I knew online in 2022. My words were misinterpreted to mean something they did not, but even more painful is that they were misinterpreted around the topic of weight—something that I have had a long and deeply personal battle with linked to my chronic childhood abuse and bullying. I can look back now and see the healing from this experience made me even stronger in my leadership and showed me where I needed to do the work to be, receive and hold more. It removed all of my triggers and fears of attack that had previously been keeping me small and 'visible just enough'.

The most surprising thing about it was the completely unexpected numbers of women publicly and privately reaching out offering messages of love and support. Literally hundreds, many I had never even known before. In a strange way, although that was my most traumatic online experience, it also was one of my most healing ones as it brought some of those childhood wounds full circle. It was the first time I had ever felt so supported, loved and cared for by other women.

I realised something incredibly important. The human experience is good and bad. We cannot ask for our next level and only expect the good. We need to be able to receive and hold the full experience—good and bad—if we truly want that next level. That means doing the inner work. The positive ripple effect of that experience was huge for me: it opened up incredible opportunities and revealed a new and important Success Saboteur Archetype that was a powerful 'missing piece' to my body of work and this very book! Funny how the Universe works, hey?

And perhaps the biggest testament of all to the work I have done healing my Outcast Success Saboteur was being filmed and featured as an expert alongside other spiritual leaders in a film aiming to be bigger than *The Secret* that will be released to an audience of millions the year after this book is published.

None of this would have been possible if I had stayed unseen and small, hiding myself because of my Outcast Success Saboteur.

How the Outcast Looks When It Is Healed

When you heal your Outcast Success Saboteur, you are able to deeply accept yourself and feel safe to be seen as who you really are. As a result, you are able to be seen more, sell more, and scale more, collapsing time around your next six figures. Not only that, but you feel safe enough to be your authentic self in your personal relationships, too—which means more love, intimacy, and true connection for you and those around you.

This looks like:

- Showing up as the changemaker and thought leader you truly are (and were *destined* to be), because you feel rejection-proof and fearless.
- Breaking cycles and becoming the change you want to see in your family and in the world.
- Feeling safe enough to be who you really are and to share your opinions loudly and proudly.
- Feeling safe enough to stand out and share your magnificent and unique work with the world.
- Increasing your ripple effect by doing videos and presentations, talking on stages, or writing that book that fear has held you back from.

- Confidently selling yourself and your services with your magnetic energy (attracting *way* more clients and closing *way* more sales in the process). Daily sales have become the new norm.
- Expanding your capacity to receive and hold higher levels of clients in your energy and business, scaling group programs (and income) with a lot more ease.
- Creating a movement and taking your business global.
- Releasing any weight or health issues you may have been holding onto as a form of protection, to keep yourself 'safe' and 'hidden'.
- Feeling more confident to be your true self in your relationships and to magnetise soulmate relationships and dreamy clients.
- Feeling ready to outshine and outearn others around you, because your desire for impact is bigger than your fears.
- Starting to accept money rather than pushing it away.

These are just a few of the results the women in the Ultimate Uplevel Academy experience, as the results that come from healing the Outcast are so incredibly far-reaching and shifting that their power can be seen across many dimensions of their lives.

Gifts Behind the Outcast

The biggest gift that can be found beneath a healed Outcast is the Gift of Shining. When you heal your Outcast, you become the lighthouse your audience needs.

You are here to shine and be seen on a huge level, whether as a writer, speaker, leader, or public figure. You are here to change the world through your words and voice.

Remind yourself: you are meant for stages, a global audience, *The New York Times* bestseller list, every definition of wealth and success you can imagine. It's all there for the taking. It just takes courage.

Here are some of the other powerful gifts beneath a healed Outcast:

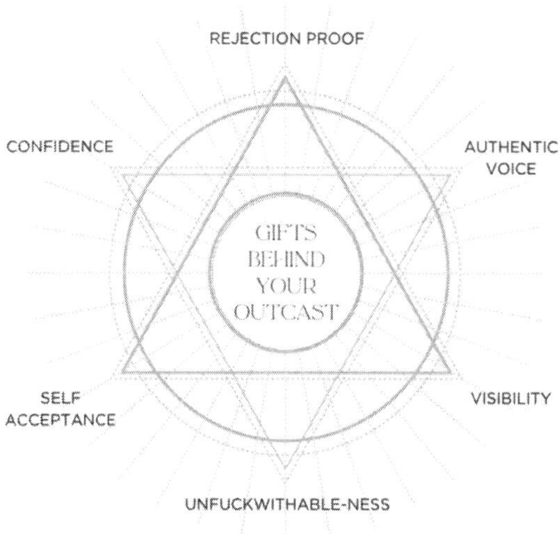

Figure 7: The Outcast Success Saboteur

Healing the Outcast

Over the course of this chapter, you have learned how the Outcast Success Saboteur is showing up for you. On a scale of one to ten (with ten being the most), how much do you think the Outcast is blocking you from receiving your next six figures?

The unveiling process in this chapter will already have created significant shifts for you around this Success Saboteur on many levels. Let's take this deeper now with some more additional healing tasks.

Mind Healing

Look at the conscious and hidden beliefs you have uncovered as being at the root of your Outcast Success Saboteur, and find evidence to prove them wrong. You may also want to rewrite the beliefs into more positive supportive ones and place them on a Post-It note where you will see these new empowering beliefs daily.

Heart Healing

Look back at the 'experiences' you resonated with around the root causes of the Outcast Success Saboteur. Who was involved in the first time or worst time? Write a letter to that person (for your eyes only) releasing any anger or hurt towards them and read it out loud, imagining you are reclaiming your voice and power as you do so.

Soul Healing

Write a healing letter to the part of you that first learned she was not safe enough to be seen; that being seen or being visible was dangerous in some way. Tell her how much you love and accept her exactly as she is, and what she needs to hear from you in order to let go of this pattern and feel safe enough to be seen on a bigger level.

Read this letter aloud to yourself, as if you were reading it to her. Afterwards, visualise yourself hugging her and merging with her as you become one.

Energy Healing

Spend fifteen minutes writing a letter to present 'you' from 'you' ten years into the future. Imagine that you've healed all your fears around rejection, being visible, and being seen for who you are and the success you have. What does your life and business look like? What have you achieved in those ten years? How many people have you impacted? Describe everything in vivid detail.

Read your letter aloud to yourself and notice how you are feeling.

Action Healing

Looking at your letter from your future self, identify all of the tiny actions and first steps that need to happen to make that your reality right now. Then, go and do as many of those tiny actions as possible, to start shifting this through little actions that add up to big results.

Want to go bigger? Ask the Universe to help you impact more people through visibility opportunities. Put yourself forward for any visibility opportunities you come across and say yes to anything that comes your way... You never know, it may lead you to getting married on Richard Branson's island, or starring in a huge film with other spiritual leaders, like it did for me!

7

THE HUSTLER SUCCESS SABOTEUR ARCHETYPE

This chapter is all about unveiling how the Hustler Success Saboteur is stopping you from receiving and holding your next six figures, and why you cannot seem to have success in your business without sabotaging yourself, your health, or your relationships. By revealing and healing this, you will finally be able to make more money than you ever thought possible and hold onto it without it all flying back out again—without sabotage or overworking.

All the Success Saboteur Archetypes impact your ability to receive and hold money, but the Hustler is the most impactful of them all in regards to building financial wealth. Its main driver is a deep need to feel worthy, and it is the key Success Saboteur Archetype you need to heal in order to not only be able to receive more money, but to also be able to keep the money you make.

We all have some degree of the Hustler. Hustling notably isn't *always* a bad thing. A certain degree of hustling is a necessary part of getting a successful business off the ground. The issues come when the balance tips too far or it becomes unhealthy and isn't actually leading to results. We need to be able to balance our hustling with receiving, but they are often opposing energies.

As I said earlier in this book, the Revolutionary Woman doesn't just make money. She builds wealth. Wealth, to me, is about having a wealth of everything: love, money, health and success. Being wealthy is truly having it all and being able to hold it all. There comes a point in your journey that receiving money no longer becomes an issue—but holding it and building financial wealth? That's another ballgame entirely!

How many times have you heard stories of people winning the lottery, and then their whole life falls apart? They divorce, they lose all of the money, and they end up feeling depressed and unfulfilled. I've read newspaper stories where they end up wishing they never won the lottery in the first place.

Their capacity to keep and hold that money and other areas of wealth in their life was limited by their internal world. The same thing happened to me after my first six-figure month in December 2019—I wondered afterwards, 'Why did it all come crashing back down again?'

This answer is found mostly in the Success Saboteur Archetype we are going to be talking about in this chapter: the Hustler.

A lot of people combine money mindset with business strategy and think it will suddenly start raining money - and while I love money mindset work (it has absolutely been a key part of my journey and I highly recommend Denise Duffield-Thomas in this area), it was only one piece of the larger success puzzle for me.

When I added the five-level multidimensional healing of my Success Saboteur Archetypes into the mix, it was like *rocket fuel* to the money mindset work I had been doing.

Why?

1. Wealth responds to how you think and feel about yourself *and* money on *multiple levels;* consciously, subconsciously, emotionally, energetically, and generationally. This is why my Success Imprinting approach is so powerful and also why subconscious work on your heart and transforming how you feel about yourself is key to big wealth shifts. If you don't feel good about yourself, you won't feel good about receiving that next six figures. On a heart level, if you feel guilt, shame, or unworthiness around having that next six figures, you can still make money and even be wealthy to a degree, but you may find it will tend to come with hustle and sacrifice or any money you make might fly straight back out again.
2. Our relationship with money and wealth is most impacted by our relationship with ourselves—and the key to healing this is found in healing our early childhood relationships, especially our close family relationships. For example, if you felt you had to work hard to receive love, you will feel you need to work hard to receive wealth. You don't believe or feel that wealth *or* love is available to you without conditions attached to it. This work on healing the heart wounds that are at the root of these Success Saboteurs is key

to believing and feeling that you are enough and worthy of receiving money—and being able to hold onto it, too.

Right, let's dive into the Hustler Success Saboteur Archetype.

Overview of the Hustler

Our ability to receive and keep all forms of wealth with ease is blocked by the Hustler Success Saboteur.

There are two key ways it can show up:

1. Struggle to receive money (and love and health) no matter how hard you work at it.
2. Struggle to keep the money you make (even if you already have a six- or seven-figure business)—there is never much left at the end of each month—or it comes at a sacrifice to love/self.

If you have a strong Hustler Success Saboteur, you believe you have to work really hard for success and wealth. Your bank balance isn't quite reflecting the effort you are putting in. Even when you make a lot of money, it seems to fly straight back out again, whether because of bills, surprise expenses, spending sprees or bad decisions.

When you have a big month in your business or reach a goal you've never achieved before, you still aren't satisfied, moving straight onto the next goal.

Whenever you start to see success in one area, it doesn't seem to last long (hello, 'feast or famine' income cycle!), or it comes at a sacrifice to success in another area of your life, such as your health or relationships.

Deep down, you want to be able to have it all, but are working so hard that you are heading for burnout (if you aren't already there).

You have deep blocks around money, love, and success that are holding you back from truly 'having it all'.

If you don't heal the Hustler Success Saboteur, making money and building wealth will continue to feel like more of a struggle than it needs to be. You may find it difficult to break free of hustling for money or the 'feast or famine' cycle, and you will limit your potential to step into being a Revolutionary Woman who receives without sabotage, hustle or sacrifice.

Common Hustler Beliefs and Feelings

I am going to share the most common beliefs and feelings that indicate you have a Hustler Success Saboteur holding you back from your next six figures. As you are reading them, ask yourself, 'Does this feel right or wrong for me?' and highlight or make a note of any of the ones that resonate for you.

After noting the ones that resonate with you, you may want to reflect on any other ways this Success Saboteur shows up in your beliefs and feelings and make a note of those too.

- 'I can't have love and money.'
- 'I have to work really hard for money/success.'

- 'Achieving makes me feel good/worthy.'
- 'It's not safe to have it all.'
- 'I can't have it all.'

  'Success/money/love isn't available to me.'
- 'I don't deserve to be wealthy.'
- 'I fear success. Something bad will happen if I have too much, even though I deeply want it.'
- 'I am not worthy of having all forms of abundance [love, health, money, and success].'
- 'It is not safe for me to have all forms of abundance in my life.'
- Feeling success comes with a consequence.
- Feeling worthy only when achieving.
- Not feeling worthy to have all forms of abundance in your life (love, health, money and success).
- Fearing that people will abandon you or judge you if you are 'too successful'.
- Wanting money but feeling guilt, shame or embarrassment linked to it.
- Fearing that you cannot be a successful businesswoman and a good mother at the same time.

I personally struggled with the last belief in the list above while I was pregnant with my second child. I deliberately found evidence of other mothers with young children at my level and worked on healing what was coming up around it for me, and had some of my most successful months as a new mum!

How the Hustler Shows Up at All Levels

There are common ways the Hustler shows up generally, whatever stage of your six-figure journey you are in right now. Again, just highlight or note down the ones that resonate for you as you are reading through.

- You have income plateaus (which means you subconsciously fear hitting the big goal because your mind doesn't know what comes beyond it).
- You have difficulties manifesting *anything* (because hustling is 'doing' energy, not 'manifesting' energy).
- Your default survival mode is to disconnect from your loved ones using work or other addictions.
- You struggle to play, and you find it hard to rest or relax. You are always on the go; you are never actually in receiving mode (which makes receiving a struggle!).
- You self-neglect to avoid connection because you don't feel worthy of it (e.g., you won't shower, brush your teeth, or dress nicely).
- You struggle to play with your children because you only know how to 'do', not 'be'.
- You have an obsession with achievement and results.
- You are at a high risk of burnout, or have had burnout in the past.
- You have a very 'all or nothing' approach.
- You only feel worthy if you are hustling/doing/achieving.
- You don't pay yourself well.
- You might invest $20,000 in a business coach, but not in your

health or wellbeing.

Now, let's look specifically at how the Hustler blocks you from that six-figure year, launch, or month. Pay attention to all the different levels discussed, as the symptoms can be fluid across them, and even though you are not there yet, you may notice something that resonates with you (or identify something to look out for!).

How the Hustler Blocks Your Six-Figure Year

At the six-figure year level, the Hustler Success Saboteur Archetype blocks you by not letting you switch away from the employee mindset of 'I should be paid for my time' into the entrepreneur mindset of 'I should be paid for the transformation'. The Hustler Success Saboteur blocks you from receiving money that is not based on time, like an online course you create once and sell repeatedly. It keeps you stuck in the one-to-one grind and hustle of exchanging time for money. This means you sacrifice everything to grow your business, focusing all your time on it and possibly losing friendships and key relationships along the way. You haven't embodied the fact that you have limitless earning potential, because you think you must work hard for every penny.

Highlight or make note of the common ways the Hustler shows up at this level that resonate for you:

- It feels like you are sacrificing everything to build your business, and are losing or compensating on friendships or relationships in the process.

- You are stuck in the one-to-one hustle, because being paid for passive income feels like 'cheating'. This means you do back-to-back days of work (mostly one-to-one).
- You are sacrificing yourself for the sale (e.g., adding 'one more client', even though you do not have the time for them or need the money).
- You are working hard but also keeping yourself small because you don't want others to think you are outshining them.
- You're experiencing success, but it is inconsistent and feels unattainable in all areas at once (e.g., feast/famine income cycle; arguing with a loved one if business is doing well or relationships are going well; neglecting your health and stopping eating well or exercising).
- You are taking on too many projects in one go and attempting to do things that are impossible for normal people to achieve (like launching two courses while you have two young children, as I attempted!).
- Your business is taking over your life and isn't making you enough money.
- You struggle to let go of 'employee' identity to step into 'entrepreneur' identity.

To grow to higher levels and attain sustainable success that doesn't occupy all your time to maintain, you may benefit from shifting your business model away from time consuming one-to-one and towards more group experiences so that you can impact more people in less time.

My client Fiona was sitting on so many course ideas she had never felt able to release. After just one workshop on healing her Hustler Success Saboteur in the Ultimate Uplevel Academy, that dramatically changed! She started to truly believe she could be a millionaire and she finally released her first passive income course and got seventeen sales! She officially broke the passive income seal!

You don't have to exchange time for money anymore as an entrepreneur. The money is a reward for your service. I used to get paid about £16 ($20) per hour as a social worker. I now charge thousands per hour. It blows my mind! When I first came into business, I thought £20 per hour was epic for getting paid to do what I love. I had to do a lot of healing to feel worthy and own my worth around that. I know that I am exceptionally good at what I do, but that is only because I have healed my Success Saboteurs Archetypes and can feel truly worthy of receiving and holding all of the success I have built.

How the Hustler Blocks Your Six-Figure Launch

At the six-figure launch level, your worth and wealth has already shifted significantly, but now, the Hustler mostly shows up in your team and processes—or lack of! Which means your whole business feels like one big hustle: nobody has the capacity to receive. It also shows up in your belief that it needs to be hard and that you must do big, long, fancy launches to sell your stuff.

Highlight or note down any of these ways the Hustler is showing up for you at this level:

- You are hustling to achieve a six-figure launch using someone else's methods that don't feel aligned with you and your nervous system, but you are too scared to move away from what you were taught.
- You have a burned-out team, and are still trying to do most of it yourself instead of delegating.
- You have chaotic systems and lack of streamlining in the back end.
- You have too much structure around the launch, and this doesn't allow room for the magic of trust and ease.
- Overreliance on launches as the only time you sell anything (putting a lot of pressure on them).
- You have too much strategy and not enough heart. You look at success as numbers, leads, and conversion rates rather than service, people, and relationships.
- When your launch is going well, you will (willingly or unwillingly) do something to sabotage it (e.g., getting ill during launches; firing a team member).
- You make people jump through hoops to buy.
- When your launch doesn't go to plan, you feel depressed or withdrawn, and you may beat yourself up. Your worth is deeply attached to the sales coming in, so when they stop, you stop selling.
- You aren't grateful for smaller launches, saying things like, 'I only had *x* signups.'

What if selling could be easy? Your Hustler Success Saboteur is making you think you have to work really hard for every single sale to come in.

But what if it was easy? What if you didn't need a big, fancy launch, and you instead just put your offer out there and made it easy for people to buy it? What if you didn't have sales calls for each sale and you just let your work speak for itself? To have a successful launch, you simply have to sell every day. You don't have to do a challenge, or a webinar, or even create a landing page. I have made millions by simply selling on social media and love teaching clients how to make sales easily too.

One Launch Does Not Make a Business

While we're on the topic of launches, I want to say: every single launch you do teaches you lessons that will help the next launch improve, and no one launch will break your business beyond repair.

One of my clients desperately wanted a six-figure launch; it was one of her goals that she hoped to achieve through working with me. She was launching the 'masculine' way—that is, she had been nurturing her audience for months, but she hadn't done any selling, and then she'd done a big launch with ads, focusing on high numbers and conversions.

That was the way she had been taught to launch, even though it wasn't a good fit for her personality type.

She put so much pressure on this launch that she was operating fully in her Hustler Success Saboteur. She was relying on her ability to 'work hard enough' to make each sale.

The launch did not go as planned, and she was understandably disappointed.

Once we started working together, I taught her that one launch won't break your business, and, starting from scratch, I taught her how to sell every day. She started doing business *her* way—in a relaxed way that matched her personality—she began to have sales every day. In fact, by the time we came to end our work together, she had had her first six-figure *month*!

How the Hustler Blocks Your Six-Figure Month

At this level, you have already had huge success. Big launches and big income months are normal for you. But something feels like it's missing. You feel empty at the end of another £30,000, £50,000, or even £70,000 month and feel confused. It's like nothing is ever enough to satisfy your inner hustler!

The truth is, when your focus slips so heavily to achieving, your work loses its meaning. It becomes too much about the money and hustling for those new milestones and it feels empty.

Highlight or note down any of the ways it shows up at this level that resonate:

- You often become complacent about money, and passion for your business regularly wanes.
- You focus solely on financial milestones and it feels empty and unfulfilling.
- You think you have healed your Hustler, but your team is still hustling and burned out.
- You are trying to control the money too much and pushing it away

instead.

- You think a six-figure month is something you 'do' instead of 'receive'.
- You obsess over the outcomes and results, not over having a life that matches what you stand for and what you teach others.
- You are trying to achieve your six-figure month using the same strategies that got you your six-figure year. The same thing that got you there will feel hard and won't 10X you to here!
- You keep getting sucked back into doing the 'doing' instead of the 'leading'.
- You have no money to show for all the high-income months you have already had.

Really successful businesses are born from a passion. When you have that passion, the money follows; it is magnetised to that passion. When you love what you do so much that it doesn't even feel like work, you attract wealth—and not just financial wealth, but wealth in all of the ways. All of my biggest financial leaps actually happened unexpectedly. The more you try to control it and make it happen, the more you push it away. Think about it this way: imagine your next six figures as a person you are in a relationship with. The more you obsess over and try to control that person, the more they move away from you.

This is exactly what happens with the Hustler Success Saboteur. When you try to control the outcome so much, you end up *repelling* the money instead of attracting it.

There are six- and seven-figure business owners out there who somehow end up with little to no money in the bank—but not you! You are going to do it differently, by healing your Hustler Success Saboteur and holding onto that wealth once and for all.

Where the Hustler Comes From

Remember you are not born with a Hustler Success Saboteur. It is a protective role you take on that has developed as a result of a collection of wounds from childhood experiences, and these patterns show up in your business—in your relationships with clients, mentors, and money.

- Being from a family where achieving high grades were important if you were to be loved/worthy.
- Having a parent who only praised you when you did something well.
- Having a family that didn't have much money, so you started working hard from an early age.
- Believing you did something bad or wrong as a child, or that you are a bad person.
- Being made to feel bad/wrong/shameful.
- Being abused in any form, especially sexually.
- Being made to be independent before you were old enough to be.
- Being overly punished.
- Being made to feel bad if you had more than someone else.
- Being ingrained with a strong work ethic as a child.
- Experiencing jealousy from a parent or sibling (narcissistic relatives).

- Being told, 'Don't be greedy. Choose one.'
- Being told, 'At least we have each other,' meaning you can't have family *and* money.
- Comparison to a sibling you felt was better than you, and/or feeling in competition with them.
- Never feeling safe to just be/relax in home or school.
- Loss of financial security/belongings (e.g., homelessness; parents going bankrupt, divorcing, or losing a business).
- Witnessing people saying bad things about wealthy people.
- Having bad experiences because your family were wealthy.
- Being influenced by general societal expectations to 'work hard'.
- Being called lazy/selfish/greedy as a child.
- Playing dysfunctional family roles (e.g., scapegoat child; golden child; hero child).

Where the Hustler Came from For Me

As I have already shared, money was not always something that was available to me. I wasn't born into money. Whenever I *did* receive money, I struggled to keep it.

I grew up on a council estate, and as a young child, I thought I was worth no more than the two pence in child support I heard my father was court ordered to pay my mother. Not so coincidentally, in my very first job, this (two pence) was the price I was paid for every paper I delivered.

I went through abuse during most of my childhood, and the shame I experienced around being financially groomed as a child meant that I couldn't accept money without punishing myself, because I blamed myself for my abuse.

At my first 'proper' job aged sixteen, I was paid £1 an hour for forty hours a week in a clothes store as part of a customer service apprenticeship. Half of this was taken off me for rent, because my caregiver had stopped receiving government money for me. This led me to believe I don't get to keep what I work hard for; it gets taken from me. It also made me feel even more unloved and unsupported. That, combined with other experiences with my father, gave me the belief that I could not have love and money.

As I grew up and eventually moved out, I was very bad with money (and just as bad with love!). I often didn't have money for rent, and would need to ask my grandfather to bail me out (even though I had three jobs). No matter how hard I hustled, it seemed like I never had any money, even just to get by.

After much studying, I finally got a job in social work with a £33,000 yearly salary. This was good enough for me. It allowed me to support myself and my young son and move into our first little home together. I also already had my business on the side for several years by that point—stuck at £33k a month too.

My Six-Figure Year

Then, I was signed off sick with postnatal depression and stress, and so I decided to leave my career so I could get well again and commit fully to my passion: my business.

That was six years before publishing this book. It's crazy to think how much has changed.

I survived on minimum wage and working tax credits at first, which paid for my son to have two half-days a week in a nursery alongside family support. I built my business around him and his schedule, but the back-to-back twelve-hour days of one-to-one work started to take its toll. My monthly income was plateaued at around £3k a month for so long, I just couldn't seem to reach my first goal of a £5k month no matter how hard I worked. Then I started to heal my heart to resolve something I called my 'relationship curse', as I couldn't seem to get further than eighteen months in any relationship. By a curious and unexpected side effect, healing my heart to receive love also skyrocketed my business past its income plateau! 2018 was my first six-figure year. But boy, was it a hustle.

My Six-Figure Launch & Month

Very fast month after month my income seemed to be reaching new levels. Every time I had a huge argument with my partner too. I was trying to keep up with the expansion of receiving and holding both love and money at higher levels month after month. Then came my first six-figure month in 2019—an anomaly in the mix. I couldn't hold it, and everything started crashing down. My health started to suffer. My relationship with my partner started to go downhill. I couldn't switch off. I started to feel burned out. Sabotage kicked in big time: this success clearly came at a sacrifice—one I wasn't happy to make. I couldn't seem to have love *and* money. I would argue with my partner every time I had a big-income month, without fail, even when I knew it was irrational. I also broke my two little toes when I had my first big launch—the same toe on each foot. I had never broken a bone in my life before!

I realised I needed to not just receive money; I needed to be able to keep it, too, without sacrifice or sabotage to my relationships or health.

Then came the revealing and healing of my own Success Saboteur Archetypes in 2020 and the multiple heart wounds beneath them. And everything changed dramatically. So much so that I had two six-figure launches side by side *and* my first consistent six- and multi-six-figure months ever since that summer of 2020.

- I receive consistent and consecutive six-figure and multi-six-figure cash months in my business, while working less than before and having daily naps!
- I created a seven-figure business within two and a half years of entering a new niche and a multi-seven-figure business within three years. I even had a $375k *month* with a two-month-old baby!
- I start each month with between $40,000 and $80,000 in recurring revenue.
- I became a cash millionaire and financially free aged thirty-three (this just blows my mind).
- I bought my dream million-dollar home with three acres of land for my family.
- I have more time for my health and my family.
- I've helped my clients unlock more love and tens of thousands, hundreds of thousands and even millions in wealth for

themselves and their families too.

One important thing I want you to take away from my story: my six-figure months didn't come from me *trying* to have six-figure months. They came from me healing myself, serving, showing up from the heart, impacting as many people as I could, and taking action every day. Of course, there is *some* strategy in building my business, but those crazy milestones come when you aren't attached and obsessed over them. The key reason why I achieved each six-figure milestone naturally was that I healed my Success Saboteurs on the five levels of healing and as a result was so much more able to take action, receive and hold all the success it brought.

And most importantly, my partner and I went on to get engaged and married on Richard Branson's island. We're still going strong: six years and counting at the time this book was published. I finally figured out how to have love and money.

How the Hustler Looks When It Is Healed

- You are able to receive and keep higher levels of money and build wealth, without sabotage or sacrifice to your body or relationships.
- You work less but earn *way* more, often doubling, tripling, or increasing by *tenfold* your revenue, and holding more profit all the while.
- You feel worthy and deserving of good things in your life.

- You hit higher income months consistently. No more 'feast or famine'!
- You feel a deep desire to take care of your body better, put your health first, and prioritise exercise and self-care.
- You can rest more, receive more, and find fun and play in your life again.
- You feel able to play and be more present with your children because you can finally switch off from 'doing' and 'working' all the time.
- You receive love from your partner and big income months in your business, without feeling like you want to burn it all down.
- You open up to receiving money in easier ways, such as passive or semi-passive income, and create assets that allow you to receive sales whilst you sleep, rest, or have days out with your loved ones.
- You manifest *way* faster for *way* bigger things. It's like manifesting, on steroids!

This is one of the other biggest Success Saboteurs linked to food and body issues (alongside the Overprotector), too. Many of my clients find their eating habits and bodies change after they heal this Success Saboteur Archetype, because we often use our bodies and food as tools for sabotage or self-punishment when other areas are going well.

Gifts Behind the Hustler

The biggest gift that lies behind a healed Hustler is the Gift of Riches.

You are meant to be wildly rich in *all* ways and you are here to inspire or support others to do the same. You've just been going about it the wrong way! You have the hidden gift of the Midas touch: everything you touch turns to gold.

Healing your Hustler is part of your soul's purpose. Your wounds have made you believe that you are only worthy through hustle, because you were made to feel bad for abundance coming to you easily. You become magnetic to effortless wealth when you heal it. Making money becomes easy, fun, and joyful, because that Gift of Riches and that Midas touch is finally shining from beneath the Hustler Success Saboteur.

Other gifts that are beneath a healed Hustler are:

Figure 8: The Hustler Success Saboteur

Healing the Hustler

Over the course of this chapter, you have identified how the Hustler Success Saboteur Archetype is showing up in your money, relationships, and business.

On a scale one to ten, rate how much the Hustler is blocking you from receiving your next six figures.

The awareness in this chapter alone will have already created significant shifts for you around this Success Saboteur but let's take this a little deeper now with some additional healing tasks.

Mind Healing

Start to rewrite the conscious and hidden beliefs you have uncovered as being at the root of your Hustler Success Saboteur and find evidence to prove them wrong, especially the ones around money, love and health or not being able to have it all. What do you choose to believe instead?

Heart Healing

Look back at the experiences you resonated with around where the Hustler Success Saboteur comes from. Who stands out as someone who contributed hugely to the development of your Hustler? How did they hurt your heart? What emotion did they leave you with? What needs to happen for you to heal it?

Soul Healing

Write a healing letter to the part of you that first learned she was not able to have it all and had to work really hard for everything she has. Tell her how worthy and 'enough' she is, and that she gets to choose ease and wealth now. Read this letter aloud to yourself, as if you were reading it to her. Afterwards, visualise yourself hugging her and merging with her as you become one.

Energy Healing

Write a letter to your inner Hustler. Thank her for all the ways she has supported you and provided for you, and explain that you would like her to support you in a different way now. Imagine her merging into your inner Manifestor—the part of you that is able to receive everything she wants quickly and easily and make huge quantum leaps. What advice does she have for you now?

Action Healing

Look back on all the ways in which the Hustler is showing up for you. Write out the following sentence and complete the sentence again and again, until nothing new comes out:

One thing I can do to start breaking my Hustler pattern is…

This can be one tiny action. Then, go and do as many of those tiny actions as possible, to start shifting this through little actions that add up to big results.

Phew, this is a really intense Success Saboteur Archetype to work through, and you did it! You made it to the end of all of the Success Saboteurs.

8

SIX-FIGURE LEAP LESSONS

When I started on my business journey, I had no idea that the income and impact I am achieving now was even possible. It wasn't even on my radar! But I did see evidence of other women making six figures and thought to myself, *How amazing that would be!* Then I noticed women online were making *seven* figures (*what?!*). I must say though, I thought they were some kind of magical unicorns with secret gifts. Although I didn't know *how* it was possible, I could see it *was* possible.

So I used their success as evidence that it can be done. Then, I created the evidence for myself!

The client stories and lessons from their six-figure leaps provided in this chapter will add an additional layer of inspiration and motivation for your next six figures—and they will also give you some insight into the most important lessons behind the six-figure leaps they had (clue: it won't be what you expect it to be)! These clients have worked with me on deeply healing their Success Saboteurs Archetypes using my Success Imprinting approach unique to my signature program, the Ultimate Uplevel Academy. View each one of these amazing businesswomen as the evidence of what's truly possible—yes, for you, too!—when your Success Saboteur Archetypes have been revealed and healed. The interviews of each of these women can be found on my YouTube channel, but the analysis of the lessons behind their leaps can only be found here in this book.

Eloise's Six-Figure Year

Eloise Burton, The Money Alchemist, a UK-based coach, helps soul-led female entrepreneurs heal their relationship with money so they can attract more abundance and impact with ease. In 2021, she came to me as she knew her work 'worked' but she was feeling stuck on how to progress her business, and was struggling to attract people to her services. She was plateaued at around $3,000 months, was hustling hard, and, at a loss, had concluded that she was going to have to completely reinvent her whole business in order to generate more income (can you tell she had a strong Hustler Success Saboteur?!).

Within weeks of revealing and healing her first Success Saboteur, however, she saw big shifts: she was selling more while working less and feeling more grounded, more confident, and having time to rest. Financially, she unlocked her first ever five-figure month, whilst working less than ever before. Within a month or two of graduating, she was hitting multi-five-figure months. Plus, she went from fearing visibility to releasing an amazing bestselling book, *The Magic of Money Alchemy*, becoming unapologetically authentic in herself, her life, and her business. Emotionally, she had a new sense of freedom from parent wounds and developed a better relationship with her adult son. She also found forgiveness for herself and developed a deeper confidence in her knowledge and her work, while building and enforcing boundaries, and enjoyed an incredible shift to receiving sales most days, without feeling like she was even 'selling'. Spiritually, she learned to trust her intuition to guide her business and create high-converting assets.

She shared:

> *January 2020, I was really stressed out. I worked my bottom off and didn't even make three thousand that month. This year, twelve months later, I decided to lie on my sofa, do the Ultimate Uplevel Academy, and nap and look after me. This January, I had fourteen sales straight with sales every day, and I made over ten grand, laying on my sofa for most of it. The Ultimate Uplevel Academy created this safe space each week where I could really focus on me. I immediately noticed my confidence increasing.*

Let's dig into the lessons from Eloise's six figure leap:

It Is Critical to Have a Safe Space

Eloise has, since finishing my program, openly shared how she cried a lot and healed a lot during it, and this emotional release was necessary for her to do the healing that allowed her to dramatically expand her business, work on her relationships, and be the leader she wanted to be. She had tried many other things before, but had never experienced shifts at this level—and the 'safe space' component I offered was key in creating this for her.

Your Success Is Hiding Behind Your Heart Wounds

Eloise had huge shifts around both her 'big-ass mother wound' (her words!) and her hidden father wounds, which allowed her to let the walls down around her heart that were impacting her capacity to receive and hold more success and money. She learned that her past was not her fault, and she let go of a lot of anger during our work together. This allowed her to create strong boundaries, where she could still love her parents but in a way that was so much healthier for her.

The Importance of Balancing Your Feminine and Masculine Energies

For Eloise, who had been mostly in her wounded masculine energy, this was huge in shifting her ability to be in 'receiving' states, such as resting and napping. This led to more sales with more ease; she tripled her previous income while in this state, compared to that which she had earned through her nonstop 'masculine' Success-Saboteur-driven behaviours she'd been doing before. This balance of the feminine and masculine can only happen when we heal the wounds impacting on our energies.

Intuition And Trust Are Key

Eloise thought she was already quite intuitive before, but she started to trust and act on her intuition in a whole new way after healing her Imposter, which led to her innovating a really successful masterclass asset that brought about incredible results and growth for her and her business.

The Importance of the Heart, Not Just the Head

Eloise had done many other trainings before and spent huge amounts of money trying to shift her business, but it was when she focused on and healed both her head and her heart (especially her heart) and brought that to her work that she really transformed her life and work in incredible ways. Plus, it made her feel more grounded, confident, and able to uphold boundaries so she could step into her next level of leadership.

Transforming You Transforms Your Business

Everything Eloise had done before working with me had come from a space of hard work, logic, and learning. The UUA took a different approach by putting *her*, as a woman and an individual, at the top of the list, and that created phenomenal results because it rippled out into everything she touched (this is the Midas touch). In this regard, she said, 'I am in a whole other place to what I was just six months ago. I feel like I am on another planet. It's not just a change; it's a complete transformation.'

Eloise is such a shining example of how more hustle does not always equal more money. In fact, many of my clients find they make more money working less than ever when they reveal and heal their Success Saboteur Archetypes on the five levels of healing.

Olivia's Multi-Six-Figure Year

Let me introduce you to Olivia Radcliffe, US-based Marketing Coach and founder of award-winning company, *The Bluebell Group*. Olivia joined the Ultimate Uplevel Academy as a single mum to a one-year-old. She was making $60k a year and it wasn't enough. She was in a dark place, plagued by self-doubt and considering just going back to getting a regular job. Motivated by her desire to be there for her young son's milestones and provide for them both, she felt pulled to trying something new in healing her Success Saboteur Archetypes with me.

Within weeks things started to dramatically shift and she tripled her monthly revenue, and within six months she went from $60k a year to $60k months whilst being able to be the present mother she desired to be. Her confidence and intuition soared, as did her business. Her company,

The Bluebell Group, has continued to go from strength to strength, winning Best Women's Business Management Resource in the USA 2023 Management Consulting Awards.

She said:

> *I tripled what I was making before. I'm not quite there yet, but I am confident I'm going to get there working my way up to six-figure months. And the thought of that, it makes me really emotional thinking about that because of my money blocks before I could only make $60,000 in a year, period. That was where I stopped and now to be making more than that in a month and be able to take that and then grow my business and grow. It's just opened the door for so many things that I dreamed about, but never really accepted as something that was possible for me.*

Let's dive into the six-figure leap lessons from Olivia's incredible multi-six-figure success.

Trust Where Your Gut Is Guiding You

Olivia had a deep instinct guiding her to the person and program that was going to help her unlock the success she was capable of. Pay attention to whatever the nudges are guiding you towards—it could change everything for you.

You Are the Best Coach You Will Ever Have

Prior to doing the work in the Ultimate Uplevel Academy, Olivia spent so much of her time questioning her decisions and looking outside of herself for the answers. She said, 'I would go to everyone asking for help with every decision. I really doubted myself. After starting to heal the Saboteurs I realised I am my best coach. I know my business the best and my audience the best.'

Stop Making It All About You

Olivia shared how scared she was to put herself out there before. Now she sees her fears were all about her. She said, 'I was making it all about me instead of about my audience and about helping people. Now I am able to put myself out there and share what I have to say, and it's probably not for everyone, but I am able to reach more women. They are able to hear the message and if it resonates with them and changes them, then there is this giant ripple effect.'

Build Your Business Around Your Life, Not the Other Way Around

Olivia found that once she started to build her business around what was important to her (self, family and friends first), she was no longer chained to her desk 24/7. She has been able to be there for all of her young son's milestones, working less yet receiving more.

Working On Multiple Levels of Transformation Is Key

Olivia had already done a lot of mindset and strategy programs but had not gone to the depth of the five levels of healing Success Imprinting took her to. Working on all of the levels was key, as well as working with the subconscious for the first time. She said, 'It was extremely transformational and it shocked me.'

Olivia's is a wonderful example that as women, we do get to have it all and can be leaders in a way that provides money and flexibility around our children. She was so impressed by the impact of the healing, she has trained in my method through my School of Healing Mastery to combine healing with her marketing talents to innovate something very unique in her field.

Zoe's Six-Figure Launch

Zoe Hawins is a phenomenal coach and coach trainer based in the UK. What I really love is that Zoe did the Success Saboteur Archetypes work with me from a place of curiosity: she had been following me for years and saw the amazing leaps my clients and I had been having, and she wanted some of that, too! She was fascinated by the results, the techniques I use, and the 'psychology-meets-spirituality' approach behind it all. An avid fan of self-development, she was keen to take her business and life from good to great.

Results started to happen for Zoe just one week in. Her strongest Success Saboteur Archetypes were the Imposter and Outcast. She had no idea how much they had been holding her back as the symptoms had, until then, been deeply hidden from her conscious awareness.

After healing her Success Saboteurs on all five levels, Zoe now enjoys many benefits. She has deeper trust in herself and a new perspective on her wounds that she hadn't had before (despite initially thinking she had nothing that needed healing). She unlocked her intuition, which now guides her more in her content and business. She has less mental noise, and she no longer overthinks, procrastinates, or worries. She has total trust that everything will work for her, has truly found her voice, and is more authentically visible online. She also *doubled* her record for her best ever launch, hitting her first ever six-figure launch as a mother of two young children, and has gone on to have multi-six-figure launches since.

Zoe says:

> *I've been a coach for ten years and done lots of strategy courses. Natasha's approach was like a breath of fresh air. I was able to come back to myself; the way I like to do things. After Authentic Visibility (healing the Outcast Success Saboteur) I came away much more connected to my story and worrying less about what others think about how I speak. I was more organic in my content, and I just felt happier and more confident. After coming out of the Academy, I had my first ever six-figure launch – more than double any launch I'd had before.*

Let's dig into the gold lessons that have come from her six-figure launch leap:

Commit To Continuous Self-Development

Zoe says, 'You don't have to have a problem in order to invest in yourself. It's a great way of finding out what is there that you are not even aware of yet!' Indeed, Zoe didn't feel she had any major trauma to work on, but she *did* have a desire to develop herself, and she walked away with incredible, lifechanging results. She is an example of a woman who is happy with what she had, but wanted more. It's not always about the rags to riches stories!

Listen To Your Intuition When It Comes to Investing

Many of my clients say they felt guided towards working with me through a strong pull or 'knowing'. This kind of rapid and revolutionary transformation is not head-led; it's soul-led. Your soul knows what you need, even if your mind is holding you back or sabotaging you from it. Zoe said her decision to join felt weirdly intuitive. Your soul may be guiding you to your next investment. Are you listening to it?

The Energy You Put into **How** *You Take Action Is More Important Than* **What** *the Action Is*

Through my five-level healing approach to healing the Success Saboteurs, Zoe experienced a new found level of 'real confidence, faith, and trust', not just in herself, but in how things work out. This allowed her to be more relaxed, detached, and trusting when it came to making money and launching something new—which is a very different, magnetic energy than that which she was emanating before. She says anyone can 'do a video', but how you *feel* when you do the video (i.e., your energy) is what impacts whether it is successful or not. I agree!

Doing It Your Way Is the Best Way

Zoe saw that the more she healed her Success Saboteurs, the more she left behind other strict and rigid rules around business and the more she let go of overthinking, overplanning, and trying to control things, the more successful she became. This ability to detach or lean back was essential to receiving and holding her next six figures. Once this was done, her mind, heart, soul, and energy were freed up, and she could take action from a healed place rather than a wounded place. By her admission, she used to obsess over the numbers every single day, but now, she has no attachment to the numbers. This trust was key to her doubling her highest ever launch, and continuing to hold and receive more.

Plan And Strategise Less

This sounds counterintuitive, but you cannot plan for a quantum leap! If you are trying to control, force, and plan every little aspect of a launch, this needy energy will push your money away. Zoe found that the more she relaxed and let go of control (thanks to the healing of all the dimensions of her Success Saboteurs), the more successful her launch became. When she was focused on service, connection, and fun rather than the usual conversion rates and numbers, she felt way more aligned. Zoe was amazed at how stress-free and relaxed her first six-figure launch was, despite it being so much more successful than before.

Don't Focus on The Money

Your next six figures is your reward for fulfilling your soul purpose and impacting the world. If you focus on the money, it won't come. After her healing, Zoe's energy shifted into fun, connection, trust, and impact. The next six figures she experienced was merely the *side effect* of this incredible energetic inner shift.

Be Courageous Enough to Be Authentically **You**

The multilayered Outcast healing work in the Ultimate Uplevel Academy really helped Zoe to find her voice, be more connected to who she was, and become bulletproof to other people's opinions. She felt happy and confident to just be fully herself. This made her more magnetic to her audience, leading to more sales.

Be Open to The Spiritual

Many of the Ultimate Uplevel Academy ladies have spiritual awakenings and unlock their own spiritual gifts during our work together, and Zoe was no exception! She embraced her spiritual side and became more 'woo', but in a balanced way. Having intuition as a tool in her business has been invaluable; this is a consistently huge contributing factor for the ladies who have had quantum leaps in my world. You can't be your true self without first embracing your spiritual self.

Be Prepared to Unlearn

Zoe found that one of the keys for her success was the unlearning of all the things past experiences had told her about herself and the world. She also unlearned her addiction to strategy, unlearned the messages that formed the root of her Hustler Success Saboteur, and unlearned the habit of trying to control every aspect of the launch (as she was taught to do in the past), and found her own, more successful way instead.

Zoe's launches have grown bigger and bigger ever since she graduated the Ultimate Uplevel Academy because this is deep healing that changes who you are and how you show up. You will never be the same again. She is a testament to not only doing the work when you hit rock bottom, but also to the magic that can happen when you allow yourself to go from good to great.

Lynn's Multi-Six-Figure Launch (And Six-Figure Month!)

New-York-based Lynn LaBorde Eastman is a private banker turned spiritual teacher, psychic, medium, and channel of Jesus and Mary Magdalene, with over thirty-three years of experience. One session with her, and her clients' lives completely change emotionally, spiritually, and relationally.

Lynn unlocked her next six figure leap within *days* of revealing and healing her Success Saboteur Archetypes in the live 'Your Next Six Figures' experience (the very same work you are doing here in this book!) combined with just one powerful HeartHealing session with one of my team therapists. She celebrated and also had her first *ever* six-figure month and a multi-six-figure launch, totalling $212,000! Her highest ever sales month prior to that was $73,000. After decades as a healer, Lynn is finally being paid what her unique transformational gifts are worthy of, thanks to her healing the Success Saboteurs that were preventing her from seeing her true power and feeling safe to be seen as the gifted healer she truly was.

Lynn said:

> *It healed something so deeply inside of me that I didn't even know it was a wound that was there. And then all of a sudden business*

> *just began booming. I was literally receiving money every day and then the thing that I found astounding was I did a launch of a six-month mastermind. I asked more than I had ever asked. I said, 'This is a six-month program and I'm asking for $22,222.' I had so many people sign up.*

Let's pull out the incredible lessons from Lynn's huge multi-six-figure launch leap.

Have The Courage to Explore Hidden Wounds with An Expert

Despite decades of healing, Lynn had never reached a core wound around her father that was dramatically holding her back, and Lynn was able to find and feel her value and worth. She now feels a deeper sense of self love, appreciation and gratitude for herself.

Accept Your Gifts and Allow Yourself to Really Be Seen

Lynn was hiding a lot of her spiritual work from the world, especially from her mother and other family members due to her Outcast. She shared, 'I would help people heal and then say [about my own wounds], "Don't tell anyone, especially my mother!" like I was embarrassed for my mother to know what I did!' She realised how hiding what she really did was limiting her. The more courage she had to tell people about her true work, the more lives were changed.

Healing Yourself Explodes Your Client Results

Lynn's client sessions became more powerful, and she said, 'A one-hour session with me was life altering for my client,' and she saw a value in her work that she hadn't allowed herself to experience before. This allowed her to increase her prices with ease.

You Get to Be Spiritual and Rich

The more Lynn revealed her spiritual self to the world, the more her financial success grew. People paid her multiple tens of thousands to learn from her and heal with her (five times the prices she charged before). She felt that she could finally marry being a spiritual healer and being a millionaire.

Release The Shame That Isn't Yours

Through the healing work Lynn was able to release the shame causing her to hide. Though most importantly, she realised most of the shame she was carrying wasn't actually hers. It was generational from her parents, and she was then able to release and question everything and where it truly comes from.

You Inherit the Gifts of Your Ancestors Too

When Lynn shared her spiritual gifts with her family, she discovered that she actually came from a long lineage of women that were gifted physically and spiritually. Her grandmother actually used those gifts in her own business too. A powerful reminder that we do not just inherit the trauma of our ancestors.

I really love Lynn's story because I am so here for a spiritual and rich movement. What I also really love is the speed of her results. She is evidence that results do not have to take years or even decades, they can be immediate, and there are always more levels to unlock! Her first six figures actually came to her within a *week*. This is what happens when my spiritual and healing gifts act as a catalyst for *your* financial, emotional and spiritual evolution.

Dimple Thakrar's Six-Figure Month (And Clients)

Dimple Thakrar works as a relationship coach and energy healer for high-net-worth individuals who 'have it all' materially speaking, but are struggling in their marriages and want more. Dimple helps them to unblock what is holding them back from incredible marriages alongside receiving more success.

Dimple already had a six-figure business but knew she had blocks to receiving her next level in money and in love, especially linked to ancestral wounding. She wanted to break the cycle of only having abundance in one area of her life at a time: whenever she had an abundant month in business, her family life or health would suffer. She was desiring someone to help reveal what she couldn't see and heal for herself.

Through a powerful combination of revealing and healing her Success Saboteur Archetypes and heart wounds one-to-one and in the Ultimate Uplevel Academy, Dimple was able to go from a six-figure year to six-figure months and even six-figure clients, 2022 being her first seven-figure year within just fifteen months of working together. The power of her work exploded, and deeper healing gifts came through her, with clients commenting how one session with her was better than years of other investments. She also published her bestselling book, *The Roadmap to Purpose*, and her social media posts started to go viral, being seen by over one million viewers. She valued her own work more and raised her prices. But more than that, her relationships with her husband and daughters transformed to a whole new level too.

She said:

> *I had the awareness that there were some blocks there. And I had the awareness that it was causing discomfort, and I had the awareness that it was blocking all areas of my life, my business, my home, my relationship, my relationship with my children. I wanted to heal my relationship with money. I knew that that was a huge challenge for me coming from a family of refugees and a whole lineage of women who have never been able to support themselves financially. You can have all the strategy in the world, but if you're not taking action the right way, it won't be quite right. That's where you meet resistance, sabotage, struggle, and hustle. I wanted to hit that seven figures in my business and through this work I*

was able to do that and open the doors to receiving it.

Let's dig into the gold lessons that have come from Dimple's six-figure month leap:

Stop Trying to Do It All Yourself

Even though she was a healer herself, Dimple recognised that she needed someone outside of her to help her heal the blocks to receiving more. So many women try to struggle alone unnecessarily due to their Imposter, and she used the brilliant analogy of how heart surgeons cannot perform their own heart surgery and sometimes you just need someone who can see what you cannot see. Let go of shame around needing support.

You Have to Claim Your Next Level

Dimple had to really heal her relationship with money—a huge challenge for her, coming from a family of refugees and a whole lineage of women who had ever been able to support themselves financially. She claimed her seven-figure year and decided that it was hers. Then, she did the work to receive it. She said she didn't necessarily know how it was going to happen at that point, but claiming it was key.

There Will Be Times You Have to Walk Through Fire

The journey is never a straight line and there were many tearful sessions where Dimple went deep into healing what was truly stopping her from receiving and holding her next level of wealth and success. But you cannot rise like a phoenix if you are not willing to walk through the fire. You have to have the courage to go into it in order to rise from it. Decide you are strong enough and have what it takes.

Overcome Your Fear of More to Receive More

For Dimple, it wasn't just about investing in herself. She had invested hundreds of thousands of dollars in herself before we worked together. It was about finally feeling worthy of *receiving the results* of that investment in herself. Everything you want is waiting for you—you just need to open the door to it. When she finally felt safe internally and worthy of receiving the results, it was as if the floodgates opened and clients started to come from nowhere, starting with her first $40k client!

Integrate All of Your Gifts and All Parts of You

Dimple had been separating out her strategy work and energy work. The more she healed and integrated all parts of her, the more she was able to integrate her work. She combined strategy and energy and began to open up more about her spiritual and healing gifts and bring them to her work.

This led to much deeper, faster and better results for her clients.

Expand Your Revenue Streams

Dimple desired to create a body of work that would allow her to impact more people and leave a legacy. Through healing her Success Saboteurs (especially her Hustler and Outcast) and the heart wounds beneath them, she was able to let go of the struggle and hustle and open up to other revenue streams outside of one-to-one. She created five revenue streams that led to her seven-figure year: one-to-one clients, masterminds, self-study courses, in-person events and a product line.

Dimple admits that there was once a time when she found herself being very triggered by this type of success story. So, she had to let go of her judgements and give herself permission to have success *just* for herself, and not for any other reason. She accepted that it is safe for her to have success; for her to receive. Now, she can see that earning is possible and fun, so why not enjoy the ride, let go of control, surrender, and trust that you can open the doors to this kind of success too?

Lucie's Six-Figure Month

Lucie Ponsford is an incredible garden designer, based in the UK, with a love and passion for creating magical outdoor spaces obvious to everyone who meets her. Yet, despite her love for her work and some successful high-income months, after six years in business, the stresses of securing the next big job, the bills to pay, and being overworked and sometimes underpaid, Lucie found herself exhausted and at a crossroads: turn things around, or let it all go? Her list of problems only seemed to be growing as more time went on. Her high-sales months were followed by zero-sales months. She was burned out and had lost her flow. Bad clients would knock her confidence. She had poor boundaries; she was overdelivering and overcompensating. And as a mum, she desperately wanted more time with her children.

But she also knew that she had the potential to do something big and amazing, and, at a heart and soul level, she wanted to put herself out there and be creatively bold. So she decided to heal her Success Saboteur Archetypes with me so she could receive more love, money, success, and quality time with loved ones.

Things changed dramatically and rapidly for Lucie. Financially she unlocked $20k months, and then her first ever $100k month within eight months of starting my five levels of healing. She grew her team, implemented strong boundaries (thanks to healing her Overgiver Success Saboteur) and made plans to buy her dream home with her partner. Most importantly, she felt deeply at ease with all the success that was flowing to her, and things she was once bullied for became a much-loved part of her brand.

Lucie said:

> *I felt I was obsessing about money to the point where I couldn't grab hold of it, I couldn't keep it. And actually I wanted it also. I wanted it so desperately but actually, I was pushing it away. I think*

you have to go through that stage in the process. And then you finally do get to a point where a rock moves or something clicks or you release something and suddenly, you know, the floodgates are open and I started making money and taking care of myself.

So, what lessons can you take away from Lucie's six-figure month leap?

You Are Your Biggest Business Asset

Lucie was no stranger to investing in her business, but this was the first time she invested in herself. She shared how she now understands that you are your biggest business asset and investing in going inwards and expanding her capacity to receive ended up being the best investment in her business. Solid business foundations start with your emotional wellbeing.

Trust And Faith Are the Key to Freedom

Lucie had experienced many negative experiences and a loss of trust and faith in herself, her business and the Universe. When she healed all of this, she was able to take big leaps, build a strong team and truly feel and believe her successes were inevitable.

Boundary Setting Is Crucial

Past experiences of bullying led Lucy to slip into people pleasing, especially with clients. But healing her Overgiver allowed her to put the right boundaries in place, personally and professionally, to allow her six-figure month to be received with more ease (working less!).

You Get to Be the Changemaker

In the Ultimate Uplevel Academy, Lucie really did the work to see herself as a changemaker able to create a powerful legacy through her business. This expansion in her identity led to her aiming bigger and putting herself forward for opportunities that she would ever have considered before. But also, she became the Legacy Maker in her family, finally breaking free from the cycle of hard work and stress that had been the pattern of the generations before her.

Intuition Is the Key to Rapid Expansion

Lucie unlocked the gift of being able to connect with her inner self and rapidly take action on intuitive guidance she received thanks to healing her Imposter. All of the answers you need are already within you!

Healing You Heals Your Family Too

Lucie saw a huge shift in how her healing rippled onto everyone around her. Her children had faith. Her partner had faith. Thanks to healing her Hustler, she was able to be more present with her family and enjoy holidays worry free. It isn't selfish to work on yourself, because it is never just for you.

Lucie's journey is a beautiful testament to how your life and business really can dramatically turn around in a short space of time. She could have given up, but she had the courage to try something different, and it paid off big time. I even hired her to design my driveway and new fountain for our home (it brings us so much joy!) and I am so glad she didn't give up on her gifts.

As you can see, this work 'works' regardless of the type of business you have, whether you are a coach, a healer, a trainee or garden designer. I have clients who have created six-figure leaps in product- and service-based businesses across the world, and you can do it too!

Your Subconscious HeartHealing Session

Now you have seen the power of this work, it is your turn to experience a taste of the subconscious healing that unlocks a new level of healing and growth for every single one of my clients.

Head to the link below to find your prerecorded Subconscious Success Imprinting session where you will be put into a deeply relaxed hypnotic state. You will be taken on a powerful journey into your heart where, together, we will uncover a key life relationship that is currently holding you back from your next six-figure leap, and heal it on a mind, heart and soul level so you can receive and hold more success and wealth. You will also experience a magical reconnection to your higher self to receive guidance from her for your next steps in your business. It is best to complete this subconscious session before you move onto the next chapter.

www.natashabray.com/book-resources

9

YOUR NEXT SIX-FIGURE STRATEGY UNLOCKED

This book has been an unveiling of what has really been holding you back from your next six figures without the sabotage. Throughout these pages, I have revealed the five different Success Saboteur Archetypes that have been keeping you stuck, feeling fear, and not fully stepping into the Revolutionary Woman and Legacy Maker you are fully capable of becoming. You now understand how they show up, in you, in your business and in your relationships and exactly how your next six figures has been hiding behind them.

You understand how the Overprotector Success Saboteur Archetype is keeping you going round in circles and only ever earning 'safe money' or achieving 'safe success' in your business. You fear how others will react to your success or that 'more' is not safe. Receiving and holding extraordinary levels of money and success does not come from playing in your comfort zone. It is the key Success Saboteur impacting your ability to hold the 'more' you desire.

You understand how the Outcast Success Saboteur Archetype is blocking your ability to scale your way to your next six-figure year, month, or launch, and you know how this is because of *so* much more than just your worries about visibility: an unhealed Outcast Success Saboteur blocks your money, sales, and marketing because it blocks deeper connection and keeps you fearing rejection. Any group experiences you launch seem to plateau in terms of your income and how many clients you can hold at any one time.

You understand how the Hustler Success Saboteur Archetype is stopping you from receiving your next six figures, and is the reason behind why you just cannot seem to have success in your business without sabotaging yourself, your health, or your relationships (or maybe all three). The Hustler impacts your ability to receive and keep money and wealth, and it also blocks passive income. Until you heal it, you will continue to hustle so hard until you have nothing left at the end of the month. Your income will always be capped by time.

You understand how the Overgiver Success Saboteur Archetype impacts your pricing, capacity, marketing, and sales, and you also understand how you can start to shift it so that your next six figures can be received quickly and with more ease. Until you heal it, however, you will never charge enough, have enough, or feel enough. You'll also limit your capacity for clients by overgiving—giving them permission to overtake.

You understand how the Imposter Success Saboteur Archetype is killing your creativity and ability to take the most successful money-generating actions specific to you and your business at whatever level you are currently at. Your million-dollar business idea is hiding behind the Imposter, and it is stopping you from fully tapping into your soul's inner guidance for your business.

Collectively, the five Success Saboteur Archetypes sabotage you from receiving and holding more success and wealth. Each Success Saboteur is the product of multiple hidden wounds that can be healed through our commitment to our own self-evolution and growth. You have already made huge progress on this healing journey with this book, but truly healing the root of the wounds behind each Success Saboteur Archetype needs a deeper approach than cannot be delivered through the pages of this book alone.

You are multidimensional, and unlocking your next six figures needs a multidimensional strategy. One that takes into account mind, heart, soul, energy and action. And most importantly, one that works on both the conscious and subconscious level.

Yes, my Success Imprinting approach *is* the strategy that has been missing.

It is the strategy that will help you deeply heal your Success Saboteur Archetypes and free you to more powerfully action the key things that will expand your capacity to receive and hold your next six figures with more ease.

Let's explore how you can continue to build on the healing you have unlocked in this book and create your action plan for your next six figures using my Success Imprinting Five Levels of Healing as a guide.

Success Imprinting

In Chapter 2, I unveiled the five levels of healing that need to take place if you are to truly heal your Success Saboteur Archetypes and unlock your next six figures with a lot more ease. I especially explained in depth how important it is to work on all five levels, not just the practical strategy you find in most business courses. Here is a reminder of the five levels.

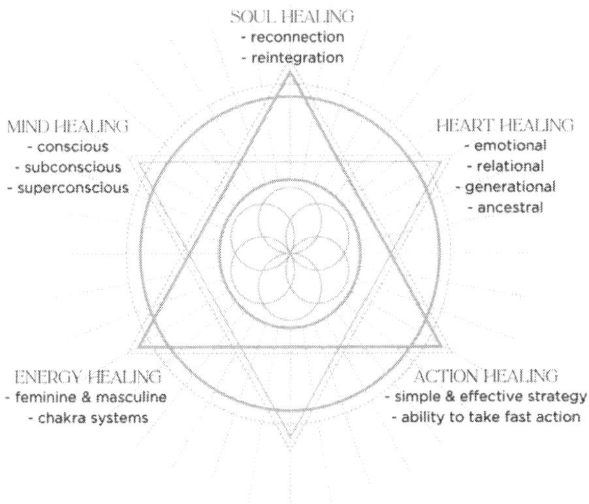

Figure 9: Success Imprinting

Remember, if you have previously worked in one area but not really seen any benefits, or even if you have done lots of healing but not seen the type of tangible results in your business and life that you really, deeply know you are made for, this is because each of the different levels compound each other and create results that are infinitely stronger than any results that could be achieved by working on one in isolation.

In each of the chapters dedicated to the individual Success Saboteur Archetypes, you experience the power of this integrative approach. But this is just the start for you. I want you to consider your healing as a whole now; to put an action plan in place to continue to reveal and heal even more moving forward.

Mind Healing: Conscious, Subconscious, and Superconscious

To truly heal the Success Saboteurs and unlock your next six figures without the sabotage, we need to uncover and work through *all the patterns and wounding behind them on both the conscious and subconscious level*. Mind healing entails doing just that. It means identifying the exact thoughts, feelings, and experiences that created the Success Saboteur Archetypes within you (including the hidden subconscious ones that can only be accessed through subconscious work), and it's about identifying exactly how they manifest in your life right now.

- How do they show up in your relationships with your parents, partner, and children?
- How do they show up in your business with your money, clients, and team?
- How do they show up in your health?

Consider:

- What can you specifically do to start prioritising and integrating more mind healing (on all of the levels) into your life after experiencing the power of it here?
- Who can help you with this? Please make sure you seek out experienced and licensed practitioners for any subconscious work.

Remember, if you don't work on this on both a conscious *and* subconscious level, you are more likely to experience short-term shifts, and can eventually slip back into old patterns of behaviour.

You have already begun to work on elements of this on the conscious level throughout this book, and at the end of this chapter you will find a subconscious HeartHealing session with me so you can start moving things on a subconscious level, too. For now, consider, how can you continue to build on the progress you have already made in this regard?

Heart Healing: Emotional, Relational, Generational

Heart healing entails releasing buried emotions and healing key life relationships that are blocking your growth.

As you know, you need to release and heal the relationship wounds and emotional wounds that are at the root of the Success Saboteurs in order to reveal the hidden gifts behind them. Only then will you truly be able to open your heart to receiving more love, money, success, and clients.

Remember that wounds of the heart can keep getting triggered by situations or people that remind us of the ones who caused the wound (even if the original wonder is no longer in your life). This is specifically why I developed a very fast and effective healing modality called HeartHealing therapy to quickly reveal and release the hidden wounds of the heart that are impacting your success.

To keep progressing with this, think about everything that's come up for you as you have read this book.

- Who are the key people you have already identified as being ones you need some more healing around?
- What or who can specifically help you go deeper with this healing?
- Would you feel most comfortable with a therapist, a healer, or a qualified HeartHealing Practitioner trained by me or from my team? Take your pick and then seek this person out so you can begin your deeper healing around this.

Remember the importance of healing the heart and how it expands the heart's energetic frequency and capacity to receive and hold more.

Energy Healing: Feminine and Masculine Energy Balance; Chakra System

Energy healing means balancing and unblocking your energy so you can expand your capacity to receive and hold onto the things you desire, and so you can show up in a more aligned way. You need to release and heal the different energy blocks in your system and heal the wounds that are causing you to remain in a feminine/masculine energy imbalance and, thus, that are feeding into your Success Saboteur Archetypes.

To further your energy healing, consider:

- How can you embody the future you who already has her next six figures in the bank?
- Are you integrating enough energy work into your business and life currently?
- If not, how can you change that?

Remember, energy is everything! *How* you take action impacts the results more than you realise.

Soul Healing: Reconnection, Reintegration, Reintegration

Soul healing means integrating the parts of your soul back into one so you feel whole again, remembering who you are and reconnecting to your higher self and soul purpose. It also means connecting to something higher for soul-led strategy unique to you. All of my most successful client stories share how this was key to the huge, unbelievable growth they had in their businesses.

To further your soul healing, consider:

- Are you still hiding from or denying your spiritual side?
- What would be the first step to embracing this side of you more

and bringing it to your work?

Action Healing: Simple and Effective Strategy; Fast Action

Action healing manifests as aligned action taking using simple soul-led strategy that brings your version of success into reality (as that is when magic happens!). It means having the confidence and self-trust to tweak or adapt strategies you learn from others and do it your way. Doing business your way will *always* be the most successful way.

Of course, as you might expect, there are still a number of key, practical things you need to do and have in place to become the woman who receives and holds six-figure years, launches and months. These things require regular work—not just now, but when you reach every new level. Many of these go hand-in-hand with the healing of the Success Saboteur Archetypes, because you'll start showing up differently, doing more things that actually move the needle in your life and your business, and doing what really matters.

Some of these practical foundations include:

- Developing (or deepening) your powerful, authentic personal brand that represents your true self—one that incorporates who you really are and your unique gifts.
- Innovate your first (or next!) soul-led transformational body of work that gets incredible results for your clients and positions you as a revolutionary leader in your field.
- Scale your impact and income to limitless levels by creating your

first or next passive or semi-passive course that allows you to take your work global and impact and make millions.

- Publish that bestselling book you have been sitting on or put yourself forward to speak on stages.
- Trust and allow support in your life and business through building a team around you to hold you as you impact the world.
- Fall in love with selling and marketing and live by the motto 'sell every day in some way'.
- Uphold a new level of boundaries and standards (in life and business) that allows you to live a life you love with people you love.
- Let go of rigid strategies taught to you by others and connect deeply to your intuition to guide your business.

I include work on all of these and more alongside healing the Success Saboteur Archetypes in my signature program, the Ultimate Uplevel Academy. As you already know, unlocking your next six figures is not as simple as just implementing a strategy, because a strategy is only as powerful as the woman using it. The power comes from healing your Success Saboteur Archetypes at every new level and then taking action from the powerful energy and gifts of the Revolutionary Woman hiding beneath them!

Consider:

- Which of these practical foundations are missing from your business currently?
- What is the most important one you need to work on next to call

in your next six figures faster?

- Who is the person that can help you with this?

Your answers to the questions in this chapter will form the foundation for your plan for your next six figures.

Without the right aligned action, any inner healing will remain just that: inner. Take action for tangible results in your external world.

10

THE REVOLUTIONARY WOMAN

I made a bold claim at the start of this book that you would not be the same woman finishing it as you were starting it. I know this to be true because I know that once you see your Success Saboteur Archetypes, you cannot unsee them, and you no longer stay stuck in those sabotaging patterns that your next six figures are hiding behind. This book is just the beginning of a new way of being and doing, one that will help you receive and hold your next six figures with more ease and a lot less sabotage.

Just take a moment to reflect on the profound journey we have been on together and the woman you have uncovered along the way—the Revolutionary Woman who was there all along, hiding beneath your inner protectors, the Success Saboteur Archetypes.

This book has provided not only a way for you to identify your own Success Saboteur Archetypes and how your next six figures has been hiding behind them, but has also provided a deep dive into the very heart of what holds back so many talented, driven women from achieving their true potential for more wealth, impact, love and success. You've learned about the Overprotector, the Overgiver, the Imposter, the Outcast, and the Hustler Success Saboteurs—each of which present their own unique symptoms, challenges and barriers, but also their own unique opportunities for growth, breakthroughs, and gifts.

You understand now exactly why your next six figures hasn't happened yet and that there is absolutely nothing wrong with you. You do not have a strategy problem, you have a sabotage problem. The biggest limit to your success in your external world is actually what is going on in your internal world—and you have the power to change that. In fact, the 'strategy' that has been missing is one that understands all women sabotage themselves and takes an internal and external approach to success and wealth.

No strategy is effective unless you take action on it. But *how* you take action and *if* you take action is hugely impacted by what is happening in your mind, heart, soul and energy.

Whether your next goal is a six-figure year, six-figure launch or six-figure month, this book has taken you closer to it in a completely different way to anything you may have done before, whilst also opening your mind, heart and soul to receiving more love, more happiness and more abundance as a side effect too. Because true success is more than just a yearly revenue figure and chasing financial success at the expense of everything else. This will leave you feeling unhappy and unfulfilled.

Hopefully, you now see, feel and believe that anything and everything is possible for you. You have witnessed the evidence. Now, it is time to go out there and create that evidence for yourself. You get to be the woman who has and holds it all—whatever that is for you. It all starts with a decision that it is yours and you are ready to claim it.

The journey you have gone through during these chapters has been more than a case of simply reading or going through the motions; it's been a magical opening to something far bigger—the universe, your soul purpose, your inner calling—that tells you, 'Now is the time, and you already have all you need within you.' Listen to it. Act on it. Co-create your next level with your higher self and the Universe and embrace the incredible quantum leaps in wealth and success that come from your commitment to your emotional and spiritual evolution.

You will have made big shifts in yourself, your life and business already, but healing your Success Saboteur Archetypes goes beyond this book. Your true healing journey begins now, as you apply this insight and awareness into your own life and business, and continue on with this growth, digging deeper into the areas of healing this book has uncovered for you and taking action in a whole new way. The path to healing your Success Saboteur Archetypes and receiving and holding more is not a one-time effort, but rather a continuous journey of awareness, healing, action and expansion at every new level you grow to. It won't always be easy and it won't always be a straight line… but that adds to the fun.

You are the Legacy Maker in your family and in the world. This journey is about far more than just your own personal success. It is about living and leaving a legacy for your loved ones and for our future generations. As you receive and hold higher levels of success, you give other women the evidence they can do the same, and the ripple effect will always be far greater than you realise. Remember, be the lighthouse, not the lifeboat. Your past does not have to define your present or your future.

You have the power now, and you are more powerful than you realise. It's time to step into your gifts of Limitless Success, Leadership, Genius, Shining and Riches that have been buried behind the Success Saboteurs all of this time.

Remember, success is not just about reaching the top; it's about the journey and the growth, and the person you become along the way – the Revolutionary Woman. You have always been a Revolutionary Woman. It's time to show up as her and change your world and the world in your own unique way. You are never alone. Your higher self supports you. The Universe supports you. There is a whole community of Revolutionary Women out there just like you and me. Together, we are changing the world one person at a time and one day at a time. I am cheering you on every step of the way. Be proud of yourself, because I am proud of you.

Know that everything is possible for you and you have only just scratched the surface of your potential. It's time for you to rise, Revolutionary Woman.

Love Natasha x

P.S. If you enjoyed this book, I would be beyond grateful if you could share it with your business besties and in business groups where others could really benefit from it too. And don't forget to connect with me and keep me updated on all your shifts and successes!

Instagram: @natashaleighbray

Facebook: @natashabraycoach

LinkedIn: natashaleighbray

YouTube: @natashaleighbray

Download your book bonuses here:

www.natashabray.com/book-resources

ACKNOWLEDGEMENTS

It is a dream come true to finally have a book that will impact the world long after I am gone. It has been harder than I thought and more rewarding than I ever thought possible, as I have had to overcome huge fears for my work to be seen on this level.

I would like to thank my soulmate, Blake, first of all for always supporting my success, giving me the space I need to create, believing in me and understanding my deep desire to impact the world, alongside being a mother and partner.

Thank you to my two beautiful children, Jenson and Oscar, who are the biggest catalysts and teachers for my own healing and becoming the woman, leader and mother I am today.

A big thank you to my team, who trust me and my big, crazy ideas, even when it doesn't make sense, and help me impact far more people than I ever could alone: Talia McLavy (for holding the fort), Anne-Marie Nichols, Carmen Symons and Carmel David. Extra thanks to Kirsty Wick for the weekends and nights helping me perfect this book and Hollie Ellis for her razor-sharp proofreading skills.

A heartfelt thank you to every single client who has invested in me and allowed me the honour of healing their hearts, lives and businesses. You teach me so much.

A special thank you to all of the women and mentors who came before me and became the evidence I needed that so much more was possible for me too.

And finally, a very important thank you to my younger self who never gave up no matter what life threw at her. I see you, I love you, we did it!

RESOURCES

Success Saboteur Archetype Online Assessment:
www.natashabray.com/success-saboteur-archetype

Safe Success Imprint Audio & Subconscious HeartHealing Taster Session: www.natashabray.com/book-resources

Email:
support@natashabray.co.uk

Our official directory of supervised, qualified HeartHealing Practitioners: https://schoolofhealingmastery.com/practitioner

If affected by any of the topics of this book, you are encouraged to reach out to the relevant support services (or appropriate alternative in your country) listed below.

Samaritans (emotional support for all issues including suicidal thoughts):

Website:
www.samaritans.org

Free Helpline:

116 123

NAPAC – National Association for People Abused in Childhood (supports survivors of all forms of childhood abuse, including physical, sexual, emotional, abuse, neglect and peer-to-peer abuse):

Website:

www.napac.org.uk

Support Line:

0808 801 0331

Email Support:

support@napac.org.uk

Women's Aid (support for women and children experiencing domestic abuse):

Website (LiveChat support available):

www.womensaid.org.uk

Mind (mental health support):

Website:

www.mind.org.uk

Infoline:

0300 123 3393

NEXT STEPS

If you would love to further your journey with me and change your world and the world through healing, there are two main ways you can work with me:

Want To Heal Yourself?

The Ultimate Uplevel Academy: a deeply transformational group experience for the ambitious woman who is ready to uplevel emotionally, financially and spiritually for true success and freedom. Ready to unlock your hidden potential for even more impact, love, wealth and success (without the sabotage)? The only place online that you can heal your Success Saboteur Archetypes and reveal all of the gifts hiding behind them using Success Imprinting.

www.natashabray.com/ultimate-uplevel-academy

Want To Heal Others?

The HeartHealing Mastery Certification: want to change your world and the world by healing hearts? Join this pioneering ACCPH Accredited Certification & Level 4 Diploma, which equips you with my revolutionary HeartHealing methodology, self-mastery, business tools and unwavering confidence to facilitate the deepest, fastest and safest transformation you and your clients will ever experience.

https://schoolofhealingmastery.com/hearthealing-mastery-certification

There are lots of other ways to work with me at all investment levels over on my website, too: www.natashabray.com.

ABOUT THE AUTHOR

Natasha Leigh Bray is a world-renowned Success Mastery Coach, Master Healer and founder of the School of Healing Mastery. She is known for her unique and revolutionary approach to rapid and magical transformations and unlocking never-achieved-before levels of healing, love, success and wealth within her clients.

Overcoming her own childhood of chronic abuse, bullying, poverty and hidden homelessness, she took the leap to finally leave her social work career in 2017, choose herself and follow her soul calling to help other women receive and achieve more. She is a living example that women can heal no matter what they have been through and they can have love, wealth, impact and success beyond their wildest imagination.

In just four short years, she became a self-made cash millionaire, running two seven-figure businesses that have generated a combined six million dollars cash completely organically as of 2023, with no business plan and no previous background in business. She has found true love – in herself, with her children Jenson and Oscar, and with her soulmate, Blake. She credits her success to her courage and resilience and her deep determination to change the world and leave a different legacy for her children than the one passed onto her.

Natasha's rapid inner shifts, healing and unheard-of intuitive-led business growth are a testament to the power of her work that now impacts women across seventy countries worldwide. Her revolutionary healing methods are transforming the women's business industry and the healing industry, and she gets great fulfilment from teaching her methods to other healers, coaches and therapists who are changing their world and the world through healing hearts.

Holding space for hundreds of clients at any one time, every day she celebrates her clients' successes after unlocking their capacity to receive five-, multi-five- and six-figure months and seven-figure years, more loving relationships, global impact and true inner peace through the power of using her revolutionary and innovative Success Imprinting and HeartHealing Therapy.

She will help you unveil and heal the layers of hidden wounds you had no idea were stopping you from receiving and holding more in your life – whatever that 'more' is to you. She is showing other women in business you can have it all when you heal what is stopping you from receiving and holding it all.

She lives in her hometown in Bridgend in South Wales, UK, in her dream home with her partner and two children.

www.natashabray.com

www.schoolofhealingmastery.com

LinkedIn: www.linkedin.com/in/natasha-bray

Instagram: www.instagram.com/natashaleighbray

Facebook: www.facebook.com/NatashaBrayCoach

Groups: www.facebook.com/groups/therevolutionarywoman

YouTube: www.youtube.com/@natashaleighbray

Printed in Great Britain
by Amazon

34826917R00132